FAMILY STORYBOOK READING

Family
Storybook Reading

DENNY TAYLOR
DOROTHY S. STRICKLAND

with a foreword by
BERNICE E. CULLINAN

Heinemann
Portsmouth
New Hampshire

Heinemann Educational Books, Inc.
70 Court Street   Portsmouth, NH   03801

London   Edinburgh   Melbourne   Auckland
Hong Kong   Singapore   Kuala Lumpur
New Delhi   Ibadan   Nairobi   Johannesburg
Kingston   Port of Spain

10 9 8 7 6 5 4 3 2 1

The following have generously given permission to use material in this book: From *The Story of Babar*, by Jean de Brunhoff, translated by Merle Haas. Copyright 1933 and renewed 1961 by Random House, Inc. Reprinted by permission of the publisher. From *Goodnight Moon* by Margaret Wise Brown. Copyright 1947 by Harper & Row, Publishers, Inc.; renewed 1975 by Roberta Brown Rauch. From *Where the Wild Things Are:* Story and pictures by Maurice Sendak. Copyright © 1963 by Maurice Sendak. By permission of Harper & Row, Publishers, Inc.

Library of Congress Cataloging-in-Publication Data

Taylor, Denny, 1947–
  Family storybook reading.

  Bibliography: p.
  Contents: Why should I share storybooks with my children?—How can I make storybook reading an important part of family life?—How will family storybook sharing help my child to read and write?—[etc.]
    1. Children—Books and reading. 2. Reading (Preschool) 3. Family—Books and reading.
  I. Strickland, Dorothy S. II. Title.
Z1037.A1T38   1986   649'.58   85-30558
ISBN 0-435-08249-3

Designed by Wladislaw Finne.
Printed in the United States of America.

To
David and Maurice
Two Very
Special Dads

CONTENTS

FOREWORD

Storybook reading begins in the earliest days of infancy when parents are holding or feeding a child and continues throughout childhood as it is woven into the fabric of family life. As young mothers, Denny Taylor and Dorothy Strickland knew instinctively that stories would nourish their children's minds as milk and vegetables nourished their bodies. Now, with both personal and professional credentials, they observe family storybook reading closely to focus on the literacy lessons underway. Because they are astute observers, they see the connections between complex learning events and the natural occasions in which they occur.

The ingenuous behavior of children captured in the vignettes reminded me of Scout, the six-year-old daughter of attorney Atticus Finch in *To Kill a Mockingbird*. The teacher asked Scout to read the alphabet on the first day of school; when she had done this without a hitch, she read the First Reader and then the stock market quotations from the local newspaper. Scout says she never deliberately learned to read but that she wallowed in the printed word.

> *I could not remember when the lines above Atticus's moving finger separated into words, but I had stared at them all the evenings in my memory, listening to the news of the day, Bills To Be Enacted into Laws, the diaries of Lorenzo Dow—anything Atticus happened to be reading when I crawled into his lap every night. Until I feared I would lose it, I never loved to read. One does not love breathing.*

Atticus Finch was a single parent; Scout's mother had died when she was two. He drew his daughter into the routine activity of reading the newspaper just as many of the parents described in this book draw their children into storybook reading at odd moments in odd places. Here there are single parents, working parents, tired fathers and mothers, multiple siblings, hectic schedules, and family crises. Whatever the circumstances, family storybook reading goes on.

The authors examine everyday language of families engaged in storybook sharing to show us that fundamental lessons are instilled in wholesome ways during natural activities. The parents they observe are totally unaware of the research that undergirds their action; they read books with their children for the sheer pleasure it brings and the close relationships it binds among their loved ones. When parents read to their children, they do not deliberately set out to give language lessons. Nonetheless, all kinds of lessons about language do occur. Strickland and Taylor highlight the lessons that are bound into the talk surrounding book sharing.

Children who do not hear stories will have fewer reasons for wanting to learn to read. Those who have stories read to them will become readers and inevitably will become parents who read to their own children. It is a family legacy to be passed on to the next generation. Family storybook reading could break the cycle of the crippling inheritance of illiteracy that plagues many families. Siblings, day-care workers, caregivers, or surrogate parents who read aloud could instill in children some of the fundamental love of story that grows from hearing them. This would have a lasting effect on each generation that follows. The authors show us where to start by giving us some of the tried-and-true storybook winners they have found successful. They show us how an uncomplicated act has lasting effects.

We have known for a long time what the face of literacy development looks like; this book lets us feel its heartbeat.

Bernice E. Cullinan

PREFACE

Some books seem to write themselves. *Family Storybook Reading* is such a book. It began with a tentative sharing of ideas and developed into several years of intensive exploration of language, literacy, and learning in family settings. Between us we have fifty years of involvement in educational research and teaching, and yet there were no easy answers to the questions that we asked. What actually happens when parents share books with their children? Why is it such a powerful factor in the literacy development of young children? How does the research support parents' natural instincts about what is right for them and their children? Slowly we put together years of observing parents and their children with the research evidence, and we tempered it with our own experiences as members of families in which storybooks are shared and read. But it was still difficult to find a way into the book that we were writing.

Over endless cups of tea, during long telephone conversations, and through numerous letters we tossed our ideas back and forth. We wanted to provide vivid accounts of *real* families, and through descriptions of parents sharing books with their young children we wanted to help other parents and children to find their own ways of sharing the stories that they read. The possibilities seemed endless, but always at the center of our discussions was our continuing belief that as we think about the lives of others, we find new ways of thinking about ourselves. Gradually our ideas took shape, and we were able to write the book that in many ways we had already learned to read. It is a straightforward text filled with the warmth and humor of the families who have helped us with our research, but do not be deceived. Underlying the easy talk of parents and children sharing stories are the complexities of their everyday lives. Thus, parents of a new baby will read this book with needs different from those of the parents of an older child; and as new babies are born and young children grow, parents may return to the book and find new insights and new ways of looking at themselves and at their families.

Writers rarely talk to readers about the ways in which they hope their book will be read, but we cannot resist this opportunity, for we thought about you constantly as we wrote, even to the point of visualizing where you would sit and how you would hold the book. In our minds we see you reading it just as you might read a picture storybook with a child. We hope you will share it with your children. Read the stories of other young children with them, talk about the pictures, and enjoy the examples of children's writings. We truly hope that what we have created is a picture storybook for families to share.

ACKNOWLEDGMENTS

We want to thank the parents and children who have shared their lives with us. Our lives have been enriched by theirs. We also want to thank Judith Rovenger, Children's Consultant to the Westchester Library System, for years of support and for her constant encouragement throughout the preparation of the manuscript. Finally, we want to thank Philippa Stratton of Heinemann Educational Books for creating a family of authors to which we are proud to belong.

A NOTE ON THE PHOTOGRAPHS

The photographs, like the text, are as close as we could get to the real-life experiences of families reading books together. No special lighting was used, and the families just did what they usually did when they shared stories. Most of the photographs were taken by Denny but some were given to us by the families who have participated in the research.

FAMILY STORYBOOK READING

1 WHY SHOULD I SHARE STORYBOOKS WITH MY CHILDREN?

Family storybook reading is a time when parents and children create their own special kind of magic. Whatever happens during the day, sharing storybooks brings the family together. Just a few minutes into a book and busy schedules are left behind, accidents are forgotten, and bad tempers fade. In this chapter we will present you with an overview of family storybook reading, and in this way we will begin to answer the question "Why should I share storybooks with my children?"

What we have to say is based upon our own experiences, both personal and professional, as parents who read stories to their children and as researchers of language and literacy whose lives are filled with families and the stories that they tell. The families who have helped us to learn more about the importance of reading storybooks with young children live in cities, suburban towns, and rural villages. They are ordinary families experiencing the ordinary ups and downs of contemporary living. They are two-parent families and single-parent families, families in which both parents work and families in which one parent stays home. Some are financially secure, while others are struggling to survive. They live different lives in different places, but whatever the differences between them, they all share storybooks with their children. Family storybook reading is an important part of their everyday lives. It is the magic of family storybook reading that we will share with you in the chapters of this book.

Let's begin by listening in as a mother and her two small children share a story. Imagine their conversations and listen to the rhythms of their talk. Enjoy the strange sounds of small voices that sometimes only a mom or dad can understand.

Jessica, who is seven, has had her lunch and walked back to

school. Her mother, Cullen, has left the dishes in the kitchen and is sitting on the couch with Sarah, who is five. They have read a book about Old MacDonald's farm and a book about mommies. Matthew, who is almost two, has been playing close by with his toys.

Sarah gives her mother one of Matthew's books, and Cullen reads the title: *"My Shirt Is White."**

"Matthew," she calls in a soft voice, "would you like to see a story? Help pick out the shoes and the shirt? Here, Matthew." Matthew comes over to his mom, and she picks him up.

"Can I sit on your lap?" asks Sarah.

"Sure," says her mother, making room for Sarah to sit with Matthew. Cullen reads the title again: *"My Shirt Is White."*

Sarah laughs and Matthew chatters.

"Where is the shirt, Matthew?" asks Cullen. She pauses and then continues. "This one," she says, pointing to the white shirt of the little person on the red cover of Dick Bruna's book.

Matthew wants to turn the pages and tells his mother so in words that only she understands.

Cullen says, "Wait a minute. Here it is!" helping him to find the first page. " 'My shirt is white,' " she reads and then adds, "Can you see the white shirt, Matthew?"

Matthew turns the page as Cullen says, "Next one." Then she reads, " 'My socks are red.' " Cullen says to Matthew, "Where are the red socks, Matthew?"

"Where the socks?" asks Matthew, playing a game.

His mother plays with him: "Where are the red socks?"

Matthew says his own words for "I don't know," and turns two pages.

Cullen reads, " 'My dress is red,' " and then she adds, "Here, turn the page." Matthew turns. " 'My ribbons are yellow,' " reads his mom, and then she asks, "These the yellow ribbons, Matthew?"

"Yes," says Sarah.

"Yes," agrees Matthew. He makes the sounds for yellow and turns the page.

" 'My shoes are black,' " reads Cullen. Then she asks, "Where're the black shoes, Matthew?"

"Here shoes," says Matthew.

"I see shoes," agrees Cullen, playing the game.

---

*For details of publication of all the works cited, see the section "Children's Books Cited" at the end of this book.

"And socks," adds Matthew.

"Oh, and socks too," agrees Cullen.

"And sock too," repeats Matthew, enjoying the to-and-fro of the conversation with his mom.

"And there are the shoes," Cullen goes on, pointing at the shoes. Matthew turns three pages. " 'My hat is green,' " reads Cullen. Matthew turns two pages. " 'Green, yellow, blue, red, black,' " reads his mom.

"Hat!" cries Matthew, pointing to the green hat of the little person in the picture.

"I see the hat, Matthew," says Cullen, and then she asks, "Where are the mittens?"

"Here mittens," Matthew says, showing Cullen the mittens on the little person's hands.

Sarah picks up Matthew's words, delighting in the special sounds of the story that make up the game of reading the book. Sarah enjoys the lilt of the melody that she is making.

Her mother chuckles and says, "What's Sarah saying, Matthew?"

Matthew gives his version of "I don't know."

Cullen laughs and says, "I don't know, either!"

Sarah giggles, enjoying the joke. Then she continues "reading" the melody of the words that are giving them all such pleasure.

Matthew, Sarah, and their mother enjoy being together. Matthew does not always sit while his mom reads, but Sarah says that he listens to the stories. Sometimes, when Sarah is at nursery school, Cullen shares books with Matthew, and sometimes she reads "chapter books" with Jessica. The children have their own favorite books and get to share them with their mother. But reading stories is also family time, and the children gather together at bedtime with books to share and stories to read.

Safely tucked into the pages of the books that Matthew, Sarah, and Jessica share with their mother and father are many of the reasons why parents share storybooks with their children. Family storybook reading is a special time when families grow together, as parents and children learn about one another and the world in which they live. It is a time for loving and caring as some books inspire joy and laughter while others bring sadness and tears. That so much takes place during such a simple activity is perhaps sufficient reason to share stories; yet there is another reason why family storybook reading is so important. When parents read stories to their children they are creating a safe, warm place for language and literacy learning. The informal discussions that inevitably accompany the story reading help to establish children's understanding about the way in which people communicate ideas through print. Exposed to loving and caring human beings as reading models, children demonstrate an ever-increasing interest in books and stories as well as in the masses of print that surround them in their environment. Most important, they begin to view themselves as becoming readers and writers too. These are some of the reasons why parents share storybooks with their children. It is the magic of family storybook reading that we want to explore with you in the chapters of this book.

However many people there are in the family and whatever their life-styles, storybook reading will bring them together.

Working parents with a new baby, bilingual families, and single-parent families with several children all find their own special ways of sharing that make storybook reading an important part of their everyday life.

Marie Ellen works three days a week, and her daughter, Rachel, is in a family day-care program. Marie Ellen drops her with the day-care family on her way to work and picks her up on her way home. Rachel has listened to stories since she was born. Her mother and father both read to her. When Marie Ellen talks of sharing books, she calls it "our golden time" and she says, "It's something that we really like to do." For Marie Ellen, storybook reading is almost an extension of breast-feeding her little girl, and for Rachel's father, Larry, storybook reading is much like the close moments of nursing in that it provides him with the opportunity to learn more about his daughter. Larry and Rachel have learned to have fun together in the books that they share, and today they have their own way of reading as they joke and play.

The Garcia family also has found its own way of sharing books. Books are read in English and Spanish. Raphael, who is six, listens to the stories with his little sister Maria, who is two. When their mother, Carmen, begins reading the story of Hester the Jester, she begins to read in English. Raphael and Maria listen to their mom and they ask her questions about the story. Carmen

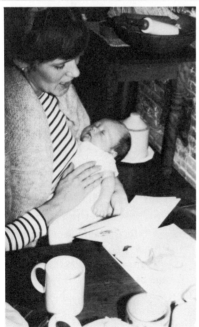

answers them, and then she continues in Spanish as she reads them a translation of the story. It is family time, and the children enjoy listening to their mother as she reads and talks to them in the English and Spanish of their bilingual home.

Cindy is a single mother with five adopted children. Four of her children—Caroline, fourteen; Ben, nine; Emilie, nine; and Alison, two—are Korean, while Christopher, four, is American. Cindy has read to all her children, but these days Caroline is often baby-sitting or doing her homework when Ben and Emilie sit down with their mother to listen to a chapter of the book that they are sharing. Cindy reads to Christopher and Alison separately, but there are times when Christopher listens to the stories that Cindy reads to his older brother and sister. Recently Cindy read *Matthew, Mark, Luke and John* by Pearl Buck to Ben and Emilie. Christopher became very involved with the story and joined the other children as they listened to Cindy read. It is a tale about Korean biracial war orphans who live on the streets of Pusan, and it is a story of personal significance to this family of Korean and American children. The children listen attentively as Cindy reads of Matthew, Mark, and Luke looking for food on a rainy day. In their search they find a small boy hiding behind a crooked pine tree eating a rotten pear. Cindy reads: " 'Who are you?' Matthew said. The little boy was frightened. He wasn't more than five years old.' " She stops and speaks to Christopher. "Just about your age, Christopher," she says. "You're almost five." Cindy continues the story until she gets to the part where Mark says, "Oh, let him come with us." Then she chuckles. "Mmmm," she says, "they're adding to their family pretty fast, aren't they, mmm? Who does that sound like?"

"Mom," says Ben.

"That's the one," laughs Cindy.

When Cindy talks about the Pearl Buck story that she shared with her children, she stresses the special kind of sharing that took place as Christopher learned for the first time of the plight of children whose early lives were so like those of Ben and Emilie and especially like that of his older sister Caroline, who lived in an orphanage until she was eleven years old. Cindy speaks of Chris's outrage and of the resigned acceptance of Ben and Emilie, who know the story first hand. It is not an easy story for the family to share, as their empathy for the characters becomes shared feelings for one another. It is a deeply emotional experience, a way of bringing the children together, a kind of bonding that would be difficult to achieve in any other way.

When parents and children read stories together, they learn about themselves and gain a deeper understanding of one another.

Cullen says that she had to "learn to read stories with each new child." Children have their own way of sharing, and none of them are quite the same. Some children will sit quietly for hours listening as a parent reads, while others actively participate, talking about the illustrations, asking questions, and anticipating the pages before they are turned. Sometimes, as one story leads into another, quiet children begin to talk and active children sit quiet and still.

Becky was a quiet baby. When she was a year old her mother, Ann, said that she was "good for sitting." But as Becky grew older she became more active. When she was almost two, Ann commented, "Now I'm not sure she would sit that long. It has to be a little bit quicker for her." At this age Becky likes to select her own books, turn the pages, and talk about the stories. She is particularly fond of nursery rhymes. She likes listening to them over and over again as her mom plays with the melody of the words as they share the rhymes.

Just as children develop favorite ways of sharing storybooks, so do parents. Mothers and fathers develop preferences for certain kinds of sharing, and children may find that their parents do not necessarily share stories in similar ways to one another. Rachel's dad, Larry, has read to her since she was a tiny baby, and Marie Ellen says that just as she learned how to share storybooks with Rachel, so did Larry. She said, "At first he had a dull tone of voice, and then he just changed and now he enjoys it more." Marie Ellen commented that she thought Larry "should read in his own way," and she explained that that was one of the differences between them. She said, "He won't read the story twice, whereas I'll read the story over and over again." Larry enjoys talking to Rachel as they look at the pictures and read the stories in the books that they share.

In another family, Lee, the father, takes great delight in playing with the words of the stories that he reads. Debbie, three, and Kathy, six, call this "reading stories silly," and it's their favorite game. Lee explained, "You pick a story they're familiar with—'It was the night before Christmas and all through the house the elephants were tramping.' They think this is absolutely great. 'I ran to the window, threw up the sash, and fell out.' They think this stuff is terrific, and so we'll read entire stories changing the words around. But it has to be a story they understand and they've listened to before. They'll sit up and just giggle so loud." Sometimes Lee's young daughters ask him to "read the story silly" and sometimes they say, "Read it right this time." It is one of the special ways that Lee shares stories with his children. Debbie and Kathy giggle with delight as Lee makes topsy-turvy stories and plays with absurdity in the books that he reads. It is a wonderful game that they share with their dad.

S haring storybooks gives parents and children an opportunity to explore commonplace events and extraordinary happenings.

Matthew loves reading about the little person getting dressed in the Dick Bruna book that he shares with his mother. *My Shirt Is White* is especially meaningful to him as he learns the names of the clothes that he wears and helps his mom with the complicated process of putting them on and taking them off.

Rachel likes reading *Goodnight Moon* by Margaret Wise Brown, and she asks her Mom to read "Moon" over and over again.

Occasionally at bedtime they will read it five times before Rachel goes to sleep. Marie Ellen reads the story and talks about the pictures. Once, when it was time for Rachel to sleep, Marie Ellen read from the book, " 'And goodnight to the old lady whispering "hush".' " Then she smiled at Rachel and said, "You know what I think we should do? I think we should finish the story and go to sleep." It was in this way that the book and bedtime came together in the experience of the little girl. Both were familiar to her, and she shared them with her mom as she closed her eyes to sleep.

Getting dressed and saying goodnight are everyday happenings in the lives of young children, but elephants in elevators are quite extraordinary. Christina is a little older than Matthew, whom we met at the beginning of this chapter. She is almost three. When Karen, her mother, reads *The Story of Babar* by Jean de Brunhoff, sometimes she reads the story and sometimes she paraphrases the text as she relates the extraordinary happenings in the life of Babar to the everyday world of her little girl. After Babar's mother is killed by hunters, Babar runs away. He runs and runs until he comes to a town and is befriended by a very rich old lady who gives him some money so that he can buy a fine suit of clothes.

Karen tells Christina what is happening in the story. "He goes into the store, and he goes into the elevator." Karen points at

the elevator and asks Christina, "Does this look like the old broken-down elevator in Mommy's office?"

"Yes," says Christina.

Her mom continues, "But this one's not broken. It goes up and down." Karen returns to the story. "And the man says," she tells Christina as she begins to read, " ' "This is not a toy, Mr. Elephant. You must get out and do your shopping." ' "

So the strange-looking elevator, filled with an elephant, which is supposed to go up and down on the page of the book is likened to an elevator that is familiar to Christina.

A few pages later Karen reads, " 'Well satisfied with his purchases and feeling very elegant indeed, Babar now goes to the photographer to have his picture taken.' "

Christina looks at the picture of the photographer and says, "He's fur on him?"

Her mother replies, "Well, that is the photographer's hair. He has a lot of hair. It looks like fur, doesn't it?"

"Mm-mm," says Christina.

Karen reads the writing that is under Babar's photograph, which appears on the next page: "And here is his photograph."

Christina doesn't understand and asks, "Photograph?"

"That's his photograph, that's his picture," says her mom.

Christina asks again, "Is that him?"

"Mm-mm," Karen replies. Then she continues, "This is the man's camera. It's an old-fashioned camera. Cameras used to be big like that."

Christina is back to the photographer and she questions her mother about the person in the picture.

Karen explains, "That's the photographer. Remember the photographer came to your class and took your picture? Did he have a camera like that?"

"Yes," says Christina.

"And did he say, 'Everyone look at the camera'?"

"Yes," says Christina again, and her mother continues with the story.

At the end of the story Babar goes back to his home in the forest. He becomes king of the elephants and marries an elephant named Celeste. After the coronation and wedding Babar and Celeste stand looking at the stars in the night sky. It is a shadowy black and grey picture and something about it puzzles Christina.

"Oh, what is it now?" Karen says as they turn the page and look at the picture.

"Night time," Christina replies.

"It's night time," agrees her mother.

"Where's Babar?" asks Christina.

"Right there," Karen tells her.

Christina says, "He fall apart."

Now Karen is puzzled. "What do you mean, he fell apart? Why?"

Christina's next question is as good as an answer. "Where's head?" she asks her mom.

Karen understands. "Oh, you mean he fell apart because you can't see him?"

Christina says, "Yes."

Karen explains, "It's just because it's dark. He's still there."

Christina then points to the shadowy figure of Celeste. "Who's this?" she asks.

Karen tries to explain. "Queen Celeste is under the veil. You can't see her, either."

Christina says, "Veil?"

Karen goes on. "A veil. That's like you put it all over your head and we can't see you. Like sometimes when you're a ghost."

"Yes," says Christina. "It's in the dark."

Elephants in veils and little girls dressed as ghosts satisfy Christina, and as her mother finishes the book she asks to hear the story again.

Family storybook reading provides
children with the opportunity to
develop language and literacy skills
and values in ways that are meaningful
to them.

So far we have tried to provide some vivid images of the ways
in which parents and children come together through the books
that they share. Now we want to take a step back, to move away

from our canvas of families so that we can reflect upon some of the important language and literacy lessons that are taking place during storybook reading.

Earlier in this chapter we said that sharing storybooks with young children has value beyond the important social and emotional contribution that it makes to family life. We also said that family storybook sharing is important to the language and literacy development of young children. As a parent, you might instinctively believe this to be true. Still, it might be difficult for you to see the connection between reading aloud to children and helping them learn to read and write on their own. Knowledge of letters and sounds is stressed by many educators and is believed by most parents to be the most fundamental aspect of learning to read and write. We would expect you to question or at least wonder how storybook reading could be more fundamental than that.

For many years, educators have known that children who come from homes where storybook reading takes place have an educational advantage over those who do not. These children are more likely to read before they are given formal instruction, and even those who are not early readers are more likely to learn to read with ease when formal instruction does begin. In recent years educators have learned a great deal about the ways in which young children learn to read and write. Much of what has been revealed about early language and literacy development can help to explain why shared book experiences are so important.

For example, we know that children are very much aware of the print they see around them. Even Matthew, the almost-two-year-old whom we met earlier in this chapter, can distinguish among his books. He has favorites that he likes to hear and favorites that he likes to "read" to himself. Matthew turns the pages of his books, studies the pictures, and incorporates the written words of the story that he has heard into the oral rendition of the tale that he tells. We could say that Matthew has learned to read the pictures in the books that he knows. A little while ago Sarah, Matthew's five-year-old sister, made a book and called it *Families*. She read it to Matthew, and it soon became one of his favorites. For several days Matthew would choose the book to read to himself, and as he turned the pages he would say the words that appeared above the pictures of the members of his family—"Mom," "Dad," "Jessica," "Sarah," "Matthew." Then he would move on to the more complicated text that appears on the subsequent pages, such as "Sarah works" and "Jessica works." All of the family delighted in Matthew's interest in the book, and for Sarah, the young author who is herself still learning to read, it was an encouraging sign of her own accomplishment.

Recently, as Matthew has reached the age of three, his interest has spread out from the books in his home to the words in his environment. He can read the stop sign in the street, and he can find the Cheerios in the supermarket. Words are emerging in everyday places, and his family is there to help. Children like Matthew, who grow up in print-rich environments, begin to assign meaning to the print around them at an early age. This is the very essence of reading.

Wherever a young child is observed paying attention to print, a parent or some other caring person is likely to be nearby. To such children, asking about words and letters is as natural as asking about lunch. Responsive adults are there to answer questions and to pose a few themselves. They care for the children and are willing to listen and spend time with them. During storybook reading, they often expand on the language and concepts in the books being shared. As Becky's mother says, "It's a good way of sharing words that don't come out all the time." Moms and dads and other interested adults help children form attitudes about books and reading as they openly display their own enjoyment in sharing them. Whether or not he realizes it, Rachel's playful and good-humored dad, Larry, is establishing positive attitudes and a curiosity about books, and these are key characteristics of successful young readers.

Reading and writing stories requires a sense of what stories are all about. Fortunately, opportunities for hearing stories are all around us. Both children and adults naturally tend to share events in a storylike manner. Since he was a baby, Raphael Garcia has listened to the stories that his mother has told him, and as he has grown he has listened to the stories that she has read to him. Oral and written stories support one another; and, for Raphael, the stories that his mother tells help him to understand the stories that she reads. He is learning that stories have a beginning, a middle, and an end; they tell about something; and they make sense. Thus, when Raphael asks to have the same story read over and over again, he is strengthening his sense of story and establishing the relationship between the story that he hears and the words on the printed page. Equally important, Raphael is adding to his store of knowledge about the world around him. Books provide Raphael with an important part of the knowledge base that he will draw upon as he attempts to understand and compose stories of his own.

As we reflect on the underlying reasons why sharing story-books is so important, we should remember that most often parents and children are unconcerned or unaware of what the research indicates about its importance. They approach story-time as they might approach any other shared activity that is mutually pleasurable. We believe that this may be the most important aspect of family storybook reading and a key contributing factor to children's success in learning to read and write. When parents read to children, they do not deliberately set out to give language lessons. Nevertheless, all kinds of lessons about language (speaking and listening, reading and writing) do occur. The learning starts with the genuine interest that those who are sharing the story have in each other. It grows with the interest they share in the content of the story and extends to their interest in the spoken and printed words the story contains. In the chapters that follow, we will explore the nature of this learning in more detail.

2 HOW CAN I MAKE STORYBOOK READING AN IMPORTANT PART OF FAMILY LIFE?

In many ways, sharing storybooks with young children is a celebration of family life. As parents and children listen, talk, read, and play, they are learning about themselves, each other, and the social world in which they live. It is an intimate occasion that cannot be staged. Family storybook reading grows quietly in the home until it becomes a part of everyday life, with rituals and routines that seem to fit the needs and interests of individual family members.

At the conclusion of the first chapter, we emphasized that language and literacy learning starts with the genuine interest that those who are sharing the story have in each other. It is this interest that is the focus of this chapter. In the following pages we will explore the many ways in which parents and their children learn to read stories together, and by so doing, we hope to answer the question "How can I make storybook reading an important part of family life?"

Rachel, whom we met in the first chapter, is now two years and one month, and her mother, Marie Ellen, is back at work full-time. Marie Ellen says that they read as many as six books at bedtime. But before any book is read, other things have to happen. Rituals have become important. Marie Ellen says, "What we do and how we do it is important to Rachel."

It is bedtime, and Marie Ellen and Rachel have been reading stories. Another book is finished, and Marie Ellen asks her daughter, "What next?"

Rachel climbs down off the bed to look for another book, and as she searches she talks to her mom. "I want, um. . . . How's that?" she says, holding up a book for her mother to see.

Marie Ellen reads the title: "*One Dark Night.* Oh boy," she says encouragingly.

"No. No," responds Rachel.

"No?" her mom questions.

"No," says Rachel with finality. She goes back to her looking.

Her mom offers a suggestion. "What about *My Little Hen?*" she asks.

"*My Little Hen,*" repeats Rachel.

"Do you want that one?" Marie Ellen asks.

Rachel echoes, "That one."

Her mom continues, "Shall I look for that one?"

"Yes," comes the firm reply, and then the question, "Where is it?"

Marie Ellen quickly replies, "I'm going to find it."

Rachel repeats, "Where is it?" enjoying the game.

And again her mother says, "I'm going to find it." Marie Ellen calls the book: "O.K., my little red hen. Where are you, my little red hen?"

Rachel joins in with her own words.

Marie Ellen finds the book and says the title: "*My Little Hen.*"

Back to bed. Marie Ellen sits down without ceremony.

Rachel scolds her. "Look it you hop," she says. At night when they read Marie Ellen says, "Hop into bed." Rachel hops, and her mom hops too. Getting off the bed to get a new book means that they have to get back on again.

"Oh, I hopped," Marie Ellen tells Rachel as she thinks back to getting ready for the first stories. Then she asks, "Did you hop? Did you hop into bed?"

Rachel wants her mother to hop. "No, you hop," she persists.

"I did hop," Marie Ellen tells her daughter. "Didn't you see me? I gave a pretty good hop."

"Make a run," says Rachel to her mom as she hops across the bed.

"Did you just hop?" asks Marie Ellen and then quickly cries, "Whoa!" as Rachel runs towards the pillows.

"Whoa!" cries Rachel, copying her mom.

"Don't fall down." Marie Ellen helps her with the pillows. "Do you want to sit over there?" she asks.

Rachel tells her mother to sit by her.

Marie Ellen helps Rachel. "You just get comfortable," she says.

"In the way," Rachel tells her as she tries to rearrange the pillows.

"Here, let me move the pillows up so you can sit up," Marie Ellen suggests as she moves the pillows. "Here we go," she says.

"Thanks," says Rachel as she sits down by her mom.

"Oh, you're welcome," Marie Ellen replies.

"You're welcome," repeats Rachel.

Marie Ellen gives her a bottle: "Here's your bottle."

Again Rachel says, "Thank you," and her mother says, "You're welcome," only this time Rachel is ready for the story and the to-and-fro ends as she reads the title, *My Little Hen.*"

"*My Little Hen,*" repeats Marie Ellen, picking up the book and reading the title before she turns to the first page of the story. Together they look at the pictures. "Oh, boy!" Marie Ellen says. "There's Nettie and there's all the hens. Nettie and Etta." The preparations are over. Rachel and her mother have found a book and are sitting comfortably in the middle of the bed. Marie Ellen begins to read, " 'Mrs. Parker has a hen named Etta.' "

In every family, parents and children establish their own rituals and routines that surround the book-sharing occasion.

Storybook sharing is a time of special places and friendly faces. Very often it occurs at specific times and in given locations, and the participants have designated places to sit and special roles to play. For Marie Ellen and Rachel, stories are read at bedtime, and hopping into bed is a part of the routine. We have heard many parents speak of such routines and of their importance to storybook time.

In one family, the mother, Nina, told us that the special place for reading stories was the rocking chair in her son's room. Nina said that when she reads bedtime stories, she always sits in the rocking chair with her children on her lap. Nina explained that her six-year-old daughter, Carol, always listens to the stories and becomes upset if her mother begins to read to Andrew, four, before Carol is ready. Nina smiles and says, "It's getting difficult with the two of them so big. They're both on my lap and it's hard to turn the pages, you know, and her legs are so long and she's heavy, and they fight which side they are going to be on, so it's harder." For this family, deciding who sits where is very much a part of the ritual!

Determining how many books are to be shared and then choosing the actual stories are also essential components of family

storybook reading. This is a time of negotiation in which all of the participants put in their bids. One father, Bill, told us of the negotiations that took place between himself and his two sons, Steven, four, and Charlie, six. He said that Steven is a procrastinator who will sit and listen to stories for as long as they are read to him, whereas Charlie wants a definite commitment. When Charlie is told it is bedtime, he will ask, "Are you going to read two or three stories tonight?" Once this matter is settled, the discussion shifts to which stories will be shared. In this family, these negotiations can become rather complex, as the younger son prefers short stories while the elder son prefers long stories.

Eventually, in every family, the occasion reaches a stage when the story can be shared. Then, whether the story is read or told and whether the pictures are talked about depend upon the many ways in which the parents and children like to share books. Both parents and children develop their own special ways of sharing, and individual parents seem to have their own preferred approach. Nina, whom we met earlier in this chapter, says that she always tries to read the story without interruptions, explaining that she says to her children, "Listen to the story," or, "Let me finish and we can talk afterwards." Steven and Charlie's father, Bill, presents a different perspective when he says, "I don't enjoy as much just reading, I enjoy more interaction."

Although parents develop their own individual styles of family storybook sharing, the ways in which storybooks are shared depend to a large extent upon the children who take part. Just as parents have their own ways of sharing, so do children. Some prefer to sit quietly, while others are active and want to join in at every opportunity. Parents often speak of the differences that they observe from a very early age in their children's interest in books and stories. The differences of which they speak, and which we have observed, are very often related to the amount of time that individual children are willing to sit as well as to the amount of interaction that they demand. One mother, Jessie, said that her eldest daughter, Sissie, had liked picture books, but she added that Sissie "didn't like to sit still as long as I hoped she would." Speaking of her youngest daughter, Ellie, Jessie said, "she would sit motionless, listening for hours." Another mother, Donna, told us of her daughter, Bonnie, "I don't remember exactly how old, but it seems to me a year or less, you know, she would sit and love to be read to and want certain books over and over again."

Whatever the individual styles and preferences of both parents and children, the sharing of storybooks develops over time into rituals and routines that are part of the very fabric of family life.

When parents begin to share storybooks, they find their own ways of sharing with their first baby.

Books are like lullabies: they caress a newborn baby, calm a fretful child, and help a nervous mother. Many parents begin reading to their babies from the very beginning. Learning to take care of a firstborn is not always as easy as young parents are led to believe. Some parents find it hard to talk to tiny babies, and they find it difficult to play with them. Storybook reading can help them relax. It can also ease a young parent through the first lonely months of staying home with a new baby; for a working parent, it can become a precious time of sharing that would be difficult to achieve in any other way.

It is in these early days that the individual styles of both parents and children begin to emerge. Marie Ellen's comments about her daughter, Rachel, provide vivid examples of some of the ways in which a young parent and child learn to read stories together. By the time that Rachel was born, Marie Ellen and Larry had collected many books to share with their new baby, but the special role that the books played during their early months of parenting was probably not anticipated. They eased Larry through the first few months when breast-feeding kept mother and child so close. Storybook reading for Marie Ellen filled other needs. She had worked for a number of years, and staying home with a newborn baby was not easy for her. Reading storybooks helped. It brought them together and occupied the time when they were alone. Then, on the days that she worked, it provided the continuity that was essential for both mother and child. Marie Ellen smiles and says, "Sharing books is not always a literary experience."

Parents can learn much about their babies during these early days of storybook reading. Marie Ellen's observations of her daughter provide us with some rare insights into the literacy learning of her daughter. When Rachel was nineteen months old, Marie Ellen told us, "Rachel has definite tastes. She always has, but now it's really getting pronounced." She went on to say, "Even at this stage we've been through several different kinds of book experiences." Marie Ellen explained, "There was one stage when she liked all little red books. She would collect little red books. So she was walking around with *Quotations from Chairman Mao*, and a little red book of poems by somebody, and then there was a little red and white one by William Carlos Williams, and she collected all little red books. Then there was the stage of little blue books." During our conversation Marie Ellen talked of Rachel pretending to read storybooks by herself. Speaking of Rachel when she was less than a year old, she said, "So she would

sit down on the floor and open up a book." Marie Ellen imitated Rachel's sounds for reading. Then she said, "This was before she could really say words. Just 'buhbuh-buh-buh.' Just pretend that she was reading." Rachel continues to read to herself, so while books are physical objects to be collected, grouped, and stacked, they are also the source of written language that can be enjoyed by oneself through the sounds one can make when reading the story.

As Rachel has grown and her mother has talked to us, we have learned much about storybook reading with a young child. On one occasion, Marie Ellen shared with us Rachel's general interest in the books in her home. She said, "If the books are there, she picks them up and becomes interested." Speaking generally from her experience with Rachel, Marie Ellen emphasized, "Not every book has to be age-appropriate; if books are there, they'll be interested." Then, speaking specifically of Rachel, she said, "Even now she likes to look at some of the painting books that we have in the house."

One of Rachel's most recent stages has been described by Marie Ellen as "book binging." Rachel likes to hear the same story over and over again, three and four times a night for three or four weeks at a time. "Book binging" is an apt expression for the reading and rereading of favorite books. In Chapter 3 you will find other examples of this phenomenon.

When a brother or sister is born, parents often include the new baby in the rituals and routines of family storybook reading that have been established with the first child.

Several years ago Lee spoke of reading to his eldest daughter, Kathy. Lee said that he had read to Kathy as soon as she was old enough to go to bed without being nursed. And, just like Rachel, Kathy listened to stories in her parents' bed. It was a special time that she shared with her dad when he came home from work.

Three years later Debbie was born, and within a year she had joined her sister Kathy, listening to the stories that her father read. Lee explained, "They would go to sleep together anyway.

I don't know how long we've been with that routine. But we put them both in our bed and I read them a story and then they read to each other." He added that once they were asleep, the two children were carried into their own beds. They never went to sleep separately. Kathy and Debbie's mother, Kate, also read to them; while Lee shared storybooks in the evening when he came home from work, Kate shared books with the children during the day when they were at home alone together.

For a time Kathy and Debbie shared picture storybooks with their mom, talking about the pictures and listening to her as she read. Then, as Kathy grew older and began to read herself, she would sometimes join her mother, reading some of the words in the books that they read. At other times Kate would read more complicated stories, such as chapter books that Kathy loved and Debbie didn't mind sharing.

Then, just as Kathy's needs had changed the occasion, Debbie's needs changed it again. When Debbie was almost five she became fascinated with the words of the story and she would try to read them to her mother. Kate would stop and help her, waiting for her as she tried to read, but by this time Kathy could read and she was eager for the story. It was hard for her to wait, and she would want to go on without the interruptions of her younger sister. So another change took place. Kate spent more time reading to Debbie while Kathy was at school, but Kathy would still listen to the stories when she was at home. In addition, the bedtime reading with their father continued, and they enjoyed this special time of the day when he came home from work and they could be together and tell him about their day.

While the needs of Kathy and Debbie were slowly changing, a new character was added to the plot. Nan was born. When Nan was tiny, she joined the storybook occasions that her parents shared with her elder sisters. Sometimes Kate would read to Kathy and Debbie while she nursed Nan. We can say that Nan has always listened to stories, for right from the beginning she was included in the rituals and routines of family storybook reading that had been established in her home.

Of course, the occasion was now very different from the early days of storybook reading that Kathy had shared with her mother and father at Nan's age. Now there were two older children listening and playing, talking and reading. We might think that Kathy was the lucky one to have shared that special time by herself with her mom and dad, but all three children were lucky in their own way. For Debbie and Nan, another dimension was added to the family storybook agenda, since their older sister

could certainly read a good story. Kathy often read to Debbie
after their father had finished reading to them at bedtime, and
there were also times when Kathy read to Nan. Nan also ben-
efited from the encouragement that she received from her elder
sisters. At storytime they would coax her to listen, drawing her
into the stories that they read together.

Time went by, and Kathy grew to prefer the stories that she
read to herself to those that she shared with her sisters. So Lee
and Kate read to Debbie and Nan. The rituals and routines
remained essentially the same, but there was a new configuration
of children sharing books with their parents. Kathy's role changed
as she grew, and she often helped her sisters choose good books
to read. Today, Kathy is twelve. She still enjoys reading, and she
continues to suggest books to Debbie that Debbie might like.
Recently she recommended a book to Debbie called *Lizard Music*
by D. Manus Pinkwater, a book that Kathy enjoyed when she
was about Debbie's age.

Each new child brings new ways of
sharing to the family's routine.

The rhythms of storybook reading are established over time,
and younger siblings are often enveloped in the storybook rituals
of their older brothers and sisters. But every child has a personal

way of sharing, and parents must learn how to share stories with each new child.

Kate and Lee's first child, Kathy, enjoyed the books that she shared with her parents. Although she listened quietly to the stories that her parents read, she actively participated in the occasion. Kathy helped choose the books and would pore over the pictures, intently examining every detail. She liked to hear the same story over and over again and would quickly correct her mother or father if either changed the wording of the text. When Debbie was born, she was happy to listen with her sister, letting Kathy take the lead. Debbie is a quiet child who sometimes hesitates to express her needs. She is gentle and kind, contented with her family. Kate and Lee were sensitive to the quiet nature of their little girl, and they encouraged her to play an active part in the family storybook occasions. They read the stories that they knew she enjoyed, listened to her when she talked, and helped her choose books for them to share.

Then came Nan. Right from the start it was clear to the family that Nan was different. She was merry and bold and had needs of her own, which she expressed in no uncertain way. When Nan was very young she joined her sisters, listening to stories that her mother and father read. But gradually, as Nan has grown, Kate has read more and more stories to her on her own. This undoubtedly has much to do with the ages of her sisters and their ability to read for themselves, but much of it comes from Nan. She likes to choose stories that she hears and is a demanding participant in the occasion. Today, she often follows her mother around the house with a book in her hand, asking her mom to stop what she is doing so that she can read a story. Kate often fits stories into her morning routine, and they fill other odd moments with books that they can share. A visit to the orthodontist or the quiet time before Lee comes home is filled with the stories that Nan likes to hear.

Another example of the ways in which a new child brings new ways of sharing to storybook reading is provided by the family of Cullen and Rick. At the beginning of the first chapter we described how Sarah and Matthew read *My Shirt Is White* with their mother, Cullen. Cullen and Rick have three children, and the differences between them are striking. Jessica, the eldest, has always listened to stories. Cullen says that sharing stories with Jessica was how she had imagined it would be. Jessica was spellbound by the stories that they shared. Cullen then says that she had to think again when Sarah was born. She says, "Sarah can be in the four corners of the room and still listening to stories."

Perhaps it is because Sarah is a roving listener that she is sensitive to the ways that her younger brother, Matthew, shares stories. On one occasion, we visited her family to take photographs of Cullen reading to them. Sarah was sick and was tucked up in a blanket next to her mother. Matthew was sitting on the other side of Cullen. He pored over the pictures and turned the pages of the first book that they shared. Then he got up and went over to the piano. He climbed up on the piano stool and pressed the keys making a regular rhythm of the odd chords that he made. Then he got down off the stool and carried some toys over to his mom, and he played with them as she read. Most of the time he was looking at his toys but occasionally he would look at the pictures in the book or he would reach over to turn a page. At one point he found a toy camera and took pictures of the photographer taking pictures of him. When the pictures were developed, Sarah looked at them. There was Matthew in the four corners of the room. We asked Sarah if she could tell us what Matthew was doing and without hesitation she said, "He's listening to the story."

All children have their own way of sharing, and they don't all sit still on their parent's lap. It is easy to imagine the difficulties a family could face if each child was expected to share stories in the same way. Fortunately, most parents are able to sense the needs of their children and are willing to learn how to share stories with each new child. At such times, reading to individual children becomes an important part of family life, and sometimes those odd moments that are grabbed from the daily rush can make a great difference to a child. A parent may find a bathtub story, a bus ride book, or some other ingenious way of sharing with one particular child.

When families share storybooks, parents often organize the occasion so that they can enjoy reading with all of their children together.

Perhaps the most difficult task of all is reading to children of different ages. How do you share a story with a two-year-old, a five-year-old, and a seven-year-old? It is, perhaps, indicative of the genius and the inventiveness of parents that they do it all the time: without considering the difficulty of the feat, they accommodate changes in ways that are really quite remarkable.

Let's stay with Matthew and his family and consider another storybook occasion that took place at approximately the same time as the one described at the beginning of chapter 1. This time, Cullen is reading to all of her children—Matthew, who was two; Sarah, five; and Jessica, seven. It is bedtime, and the family is sitting on the floor in the bedroom that Jessica and Sarah share. Jessica has visited the school library and has brought home *Chester Cricket's Pigeon Ride* by George Selden. Jessica is ready to read the story, and Sarah quickly joins her mother and older sister. Matthew is playing. Sarah calls him: "Matthew! We're going to have a ride!" Matthew runs over to his mom, and together they look for Chester Cricket in the picture on the cover of the book. As they prepare for the story Cullen, Jessica, and Sarah try to engage Matthew's interest in the story that they are going to share. Cullen asks him, "Where's the pigeon?" and when he points to the pigeon, Jessica says, "Good boy!" Then, while Jessica holds Matthew's attention, Cullen talks with Sarah about the drawings in the book. A complicated to-and-fro takes place as Cullen orchestrates multiple conversations with her children. Then Matthew shouts, "A cat!" and the conversation about the illustrations is punctuated by his cries as he shouts, "A cat! A cat!" over and over again, until, with a simple "O.K.," Cullen brings the children together and she begins to read the story.

Sharing storybooks enables parents and children to create their own family story.

Cullen says about sharing stories, "It is a good way to pull all the loose ends together." Those who study language development have made us very much aware of the importance of the social context in which children learn language and use language to learn. They tell us that these social situations almost always involve people, activities, talk, and feelings. Family storybook sharing is a social activity in which people are involved in an intimate exchange of ideas and feelings. How Rachel and her mother get ready for story sharing is an excellent example of the social context in which a child's language and thinking flourish. In each of the story-sharing occasions described in this chapter, the feelings and reactions of the parents and children are infinitely more important than the book reading itself. These reactions and feelings help children to build an understanding of themselves as members of families and as individuals in a social world.

As we have seen, the conversations surrounding storybook sharing can inform us about how a child is developing. Rachel tests her ability to use language to negotiate with her mom. Carol and Andrew count on Nina's sense of fairness as they vie for a place on her lap. Very different personalities emerge as Charlie and Steven approach storytime with their father, Bill. Their father is sensitive to these differences and recognizes that how they are dealt with has an affect on the sharing. Then, when new children enter the family, the occasion changes. There is a mutual adjustment to be made. Parents and older siblings adapt to the new child's needs, and the newcomer gradually learns how to fit in.

Storybook sharing is one part of a broad socialization process. It provides an important occasion through which children learn language, play with ideas, and build trust and understanding as they learn about life within the family and about life in the world beyond.

3 HOW WILL FAMILY STORYBOOK SHARING HELP MY CHILD TO READ AND WRITE?

For many families, storybook sharing is such a natural part of daily life that parents rarely spend much time actually planning for it or reflecting on its value. They simply do it. As we have mentioned before, that is probably what makes it work. Nevertheless, parents are naturally concerned about their children's educational future, and they want to know more about how family experiences of storybook reading can benefit their children as they learn to read and write in the more formal environment of the first-grade classroom. We acknowledge and support parents in this concern, and we agree that there are some advantages to stepping back from the situation and taking a look at what appears to be happening. Thus, as we try to answer the question "How will family storybook sharing help my child to read and write?", we hope to show how these family experiences can benefit children as they learn both socially and intellectually.

James is sick. He has a bad cough and a fever. Donna, his mother, is sharing storybooks with him, and they are playing his favorite game. James is almost three and he has listened to the story *Goodnight Moon*, by Margaret Wise Brown, many times. He knows the words of the text and is ready to play the game of finding the mouse that is hidden in the pictures that accompany the text. (In the pictures that Clement Hurd made to go with the story, there is a mouse that appears in the red and green bedroom of the little bunny that is supposed to be going to sleep.) In the game that James and his mother play, James tries to find the tricky little mouse that hides in different places about the room.

James has just turned the page to a new picture of the red and green room, and he studies it carefully. "Where?" he asks

34

*How Will Fam-
ily Storybook
Sharing Help
My Child to
Read and
Write?*

his mom as he looks for the mouse. "Where, Mom?"

Donna waits a moment. "Do you want me to give you a hint?" she says.

James takes a breath, thrusts out his hand, and points. He has found the mouse.

Donna laughs, "You've found him!"

James laughs with his mom and turns the page. There in front of him are two black-and-white pictures of things that appear in the red and green room. "Goodnight," James says, and then, using the words of the text, he "reads," " 'Goodnight kittens.' "

Donna reads it after him: " 'Goodnight kittens.' "

James looks at the next page and "reads" the next line of the text. " 'Goodnight mittens,' " he says.

"Goodnight," Donna adds.

James turns the page and there is another version of the brightly lit red and green room. James is back to the game. "Where's mouse now?" he asks his mother as he looks intently at the picture.

Donna watches, smiling at James.

James looks puzzled and puts his face closer to the picture of the room. "I don't know," he says, almost to himself. He looks at Donna and asks, "Where, Mom?"

Donna is enjoying playing with James. "Shall I give you a hint?" she asks him.

"Yeah!" says James, grinning at his mom.

"It's over somewhere on this page," Donna tells him.

"Where?" asks James, looking seriously at the picture of the brightly lit fireplace and the moon peeping in the window.

"He climbed on top of something," Donna says, offering another clue.

"What?" questions James as he explores both pages.

"Well," Donna coaxes James, "look carefully." She waits a few seconds and then she points to one side of the picture. "He's not on this side," she tells him. "Look on this page," she advises.

James looks at the page and makes a sizzling noise, "Szzz!" and points to the mouse that is on the top of the bookshelves behind the old lady who whispers, "Hush."

Donna laughs and James laughs with her as he turns the page to the black-and-white pictures of things that appear in the red and green room. "Goodnight house," says James as he returns to the story in the book.

"Goodnight mouse," says James as he looks at the little grey mouse on the next page.

" 'And goodnight mouse,' " reads Donna.

James turns the page and there again is another view of the red and green room with the brightly lit fireplace and the bunny in bed.

"Where is mouse now?" James asks his mom. Smiling, he looks up at her and says, "Give me a hint."

James is flushed with a fever but his eyes are bright with the merriment that comes of sharing a special game with his mother. Donna has also enjoyed the game; as a working parent, these precious moments are especially important. Her pleasure is just being with him. Intuitively, Donna knows that James is learning as they play, but we would hazard a guess that as Donna plays with James she is not thinking particularly of the educational value of the game. And yet she is creating a learning environment for James through which everyday experiences of the language of books are becoming a part of the unfolding life of the family. Donna is effectively optimizing the opportunities that James has to learn.

What evidence do we have that James is actually learning? First of all, James likes the story that he is sharing with his mom. He has listened to the story many times. He is familiar with the language of the story, so familiar that he is willing to experiment and play the game with her. He can study the pictures, listen to his mother as she gives him hints about finding the mouse, think about what she has said, actively search for the mouse, find it, laugh with his mom and enjoy the game, turn the page and say the story line, and then turn the page and find the mouse again. He is observing, listening, thinking, talking, and playing. There are very few (if any) formal activities that could improve upon the opportunities that James has here for learning in such a pleasurable way. Certainly no workbook page could compete with the value of the informal learning that is taking place as James and his mother play together.

Family experiences with books and stories help children to build a storehouse of information that they will need as they learn to read and write.

In the previous chapters we met Rachel when she was two and three years of age. Let's go back for a moment to when she was just six to nine months of age and look at the stories that Marie Ellen and Larry shared with her. The titles give us a good idea of what the books were about: *Things I Like to Eat, Things I Like to Look At, Things I Like to Wear,* and *Things I Like to Play With.* The books formed a framework for Marie Ellen and Larry that helped them to share with Rachel the daily experiences that were so important in her young life. But best of all, Rachel liked to listen as her parents talked and read about the familiar things that appeared upon the pages of her books.

Other books that Rachel listened to introduced her to the world outside of her own family and her own experiences of everyday life. One such book was *Animals in the Country* and another was *I Am a Puppy.* Rachel listened to *I Am a Puppy* many times during her first year of life, and each time her mom or dad read the story they shared it a little differently as they related the tale to the things that were happening to Rachel.

When Rachel was six months old, this is the way that Marie Ellen shared the book with her.

" 'I am a puppy,' " Marie Ellen reads, playing with the sounds of the words as she reads the title of the book to Rachel. " 'My name is Bruno. I am a beagle.' "

Rachel gurgles appreciatively.

"Yeah," says Marie Ellen, responding to her daughter. She continues talking to Rachel as she tells her about the story. "Bruno lives in the country, right?" She points at the picture. "See his house? And there's a big field of grass."

Marie Ellen returns to the story: " 'I like to play with my friends. We run across the fields. Sometimes we wrestle and roll around. Whenever I find something nice I bring it home.' "

She stops reading and speaks to Rachel: "He's found an old shoe."

Rachel makes a sound that sounds a little like "Yeah."

"Yeah," says her mom before she continues the story. " 'In the summer I swim in the creek.' "

Again she stops. "See him swimming with a turtle and a frog?"

" 'In winter I play in the snow.' "

Marie Ellen points to the picture. "He's chasing the bunny. See the bunny rabbit?" she asks Rachel.

Rachel makes her "Yeah" sound.

" 'Best of all I like to explore,' " her mom reads. " 'I like to explore. I creep through bushes. I crawl through rocks.' "

Marie Ellen stops again to talk to Rachel. "And what does he do? He sniffs." She makes snuffling, sniffing noises, imitating Bruno.

37

*How Will Fam-
ily Storybook
Sharing Help
My Child to
Read and
Write?*

" 'Once I met a skunk,' " Marie Ellen reads on quickly. " 'Luck-ily he was friendly. Once I met some big dogs. They turned out to be friendly too.' " She stops and says, "Yeah."

"Yeah, yeah, yeah," adds Rachel.

" 'Every time I get myself dirty I have to take a bath.' "

"Yeah," says Rachel.

" 'I hate baths,' " reads her mom, and then to Rachel she says, "Rachel likes her bath."

Marie Ellen finishes the story: " 'And every night I curl up in my bed and go to sleep.' "

As Rachel listens to the story her world expands to fields and meadows, beagles and bunnies. She learns of new places and new things to do. Perhaps much of what she is told is beyond her understanding, but her mother is talking to her and she listens. She hears many new words as she is introduced to the world outside of her own family, and she is learning to make connections between the symbolic world of books and her ex-periences of everyday life.

Two months later, with many readings in between, Marie Ellen read the story again to Rachel. It is the same story, but the way it is shared reflects the changes that are taking place in Rachel's young life. Marie Ellen finds new things in the story to talk about and new ways to connect the story with Rachel's own experiences.

She talks about Bruno running in the fields, about wrestling in the grass and flowers, about the little bird and the field mice that watch Bruno, and about chasing bunnies. Marie Ellen talks about baths again, only this time she shows Rachel the picture and she tells her that Bruno takes off his collar just as she takes off her clothes when she is getting ready for a bath. In this particular sharing of the story, another kind of connection is made for Rachel. This time it is between books as Marie Ellen links the story of Bruno with another book that they have shared. When she reaches the place in the story where Bruno is chasing a bunny, she says to Rachel, "See the bunny." And then she reminds her of another book: "Remember there were bunnies on the cover of *Animals in the Country?*"

Later, another connection is made when Rachel and her mother read a book about puppies. Marie Ellen reads, " 'Puppies are sometimes small and sometimes big.' " She shows the puppies to Rachel: "See the big puppy?" Then she reads, " 'And always playful,' " adding "Like our friend Bruno." In this story Rachel is also introduced to such concepts as big, small, playful, noisy, hungry, and naughty.

New words, new concepts, and new connections are all part of family storybook sharing. It is one way that parents have of making meaning to the infant and child, and a way that they can help their children to learn the whys and wherefores of everyday life. Connections are made between books and between lives so that eventually real-life experiences can be related to stories that have been read and new understandings can develop. Sometimes the tasks that children try to accomplish seem almost insurmountable, but how helpful it is when there is a story to remember. For Steven, whom we have mentioned in the previous chapter, the story that helped him as he learned new things was the story of the Little Engine That Could: "I think I can. I think I can."

In this section we have shared the stories that were read to a very young child. These are the beginnings of family storybook experiences. As children grow we can almost see them learning as we observe them asking questions about the people, places, and things that they meet in the pages of the books that we share. We can watch them as they themselves begin to make connections between what they have learned in books and their own personal experiences. If we listen, we will hear an increasing use of book-related words as they talk more and more about books and stories. These experiences help young children as they learn to read and write.

Sharing storybooks helps children develop a sense of how stories are constructed, an important step in learning to read and write.

Children who have a concept of what makes a story are more apt to develop an understanding of stories written by others and the ability to create their own. One of the ways that parents can observe their children as they learn the structure of stories is simply to listen to them as they learn to read for themselves.

Listen to Matthew when he was just three, "reading" to his mother. The book is *Are You My Mother?* by P. D. Eastman. It is the story of a baby bird that goes in search of his mother. But as he has never seen her he is not sure what she looks like and so the fun begins.

"Up down up down

"Away he went.

"Down the baby bird went."

Matthew turns the page: " 'He came to a kitten.' " He stops "reading" and looks at his mom. "Now?" he asks as he tries to work out if he is on the right page. "This one. Now this one. Or this one?"

"Here we are," Cullen says as she helps him find the kitten page.

"He came to a kitty," Matthew "reads."

" 'Are you my mother?' he said to the kitty.

" 'No. I'm a cat.'

"The kitty wasn't his mother so he went on.

" 'Are you my mother?' he said to the hen.

" 'No. I'm a hen.'

"The kitten. The kitten and the hen were not his mother. He went on."

Matthew turns the page and says to his mother, "Is this it?"

"Hmm-hmm," Cullen replies.

"O.K. He came to a dog.

" 'Are you my mother?' said the dog.

" 'No, I'm a dog.'

"So he came to a cow.

" 'Are you my mother?' said the cow.

" 'No. I'm a cow.' "

Matthew stops "reading." "You read this," he tells his mom as he turns back through the pages.

Cullen begins to read: " 'So the baby bird went on.' "

"I said that," Matthew tells her.

"Yes. O.K. And then ' "Are you my mother?" he said to the cow.' "

"I just—I said that."

"O.K. 'The kitten and the hen were not his mother.' "

"No," Matthew says, and then with great feeling he demonstrates how the line should be read. " 'The kitten and the hen were not his mother!' "

Matthew continues, "The dog and the cow not his mother. 'I had a mother! I have to find her!' He ran and he went on." Matthew speeds up. "He saw a boat. He stopped. He waved. It went on. He saw a big crane."

Matthew begins to speak in a high-pitched voice like a baby bird: " 'Here I am, mother!' The crane didn't stop. He went on. The crane went on."

Matthew and his mother continue until they reach the end of the story. Then, while she is busy with other things, he begins again:

"Egg jumped

" 'I think my baby bird'—

"Jumped jumped and jumped and jumped

"Out came the baby bird!

" 'Where is my mother?'

"He looked up.

"He didn't see her.

"He looked down.

"He didn't see her."

In Matthew's reading we can observe him as he works at gaining an understanding of the sense of story, which is so vital to all young children as they learn to read and write. Much of the talk between Matthew and his mom has to do with handling the book, finding the page, matching the picture to the text, and getting the right sound to the words of the story. Matthew is learning to talk about language as well as to use it. Again we can observe his progress as he learns to reflect and to analyze the forms of written language. These too, are skills that will help him as he encounters the language of language instruction when he is taught more about reading and writing in school.

In the previous chapter we looked closely at the ways in which children learn about one another through the stories that they share with their brothers and sisters. In this chapter we want to emphasize that it is the children themselves who explore the structure of stories as they read to one another. At about the time that Matthew shared *Are You My Mother?* with his mother, he shared another book with his sister Sarah, who was then in kindergarten. The book that Sarah and Matthew shared was *Dear Zoo* by Rod Campbell. In the story a child writes to a zoo and asks for a pet. On the first page the story line goes as follows:

I wrote to the zoo
to send me a pet.
They sent me an . . .

On the next page is a flap that resembles a large yellow crate. On it is a tag that states, "From the Zoo." The crate opens and there inside is an elephant. The child says "Elephant" and then continues with the lines that follow:

He was too big!
So I sent him back.

Cullen has read the story to Sarah and Matthew, and Sarah has learned to read the story for herself. She is in that in-between stage, reading some words and saying others from memory.

When Sarah reads, Matthew likes to join in. During one reading, Sarah reads the first page about the elephant, and Matthew joins in on the second.

Sarah turns the page and reads, " 'So they sent me a . . .' " She opens the crate.

"Giraffe," says Matthew.

Sarah also says, "Giraffe," and she reads the line beneath the crate: " 'He was too tall!' "

"Tall," echos Matthew.

" 'I sent him back.' " Sarah finishes the page.

Sarah and Matthew continue reading together until they reach the last page. Sarah begins, approximating the words of the story, "So the zoo thought. They thought and thought and thought. They sent me . . .' "

Matthew joins in and says "sent me" with Sarah.

" 'A . . .' " reads Sarah.

Together the children say, ". . . doggy."

" 'He was . . .' " Sarah begins.

". . . just right," Matthew quickly adds.

"Right," says Sarah.

"I kept him," Matthew continues.

Sarah joins in with "kept him," and then she pauses, studying the page. " 'He was perfect,' " she reads. " 'I kept him.' "

Cullen says, "Mmm-mmm."

Sarah goes on positively, " 'He was perfect.' Matthew. 'I kept him.' That's it. The end."

When Sarah has finished reading the book, Cullen asks Matthew if he would like to read it. Matthew does, and again we are going to focus on the ending of the story.

Matthew talks the written story and occasionally Sarah gives him hints. But most of the time he is reading on his own:

" 'Then they thought and thought.

" 'Then they brought me a doggy

" 'So I kept him

" 'He was just right

" 'He was just right

" 'He was perfect.' "

Sarah interjects, " 'I kept him,' " which is the line that follows "He was perfect."

" 'I kept him!' " shouts Matthew; then he bursts out, "The end!"

Again we can see that, as Sarah and Matthew engage in reading *Dear Zoo*, they are exploring the structure of stories in a way that is meaningful to them. Getting the ending "right" is not easy. It takes time. Fortunately for Sarah and Matthew, their learning task is not formally structured. They are learning as they are playing.

In family situations where busy schedules rush the day, a parent might miss the learning that is taking place when children engage in story talk. However, when parents spend even brief moments observing and reflecting on what is happening, they easily develop an ear for their own children's learning. Through observation they become aware that the sense of story that their children are developing is a vital part of the process of learning to read and write.

Family storybook reading provides children with a treasury of words that can be listened to and talked about as multiple readings reinforce and extend their meaning.

There is no doubt that engagement in storybook reading is one of the richest resources for vocabulary development available to children.

When Rachel was six months old her mother shared a book with her about babies. Marie Ellen talks for her daughter, holding conversations with her as they read the book together.

"Shall we read that book together?

" '*Families.*'

"There's two babies on the front cover.

"Yeah.

"It's nice to look at pictures, isn't it?

"Yeah.

" 'Mother. Mother and baby.'

"Where's the baby? Show me the baby. Here's the baby.

" 'Father'—Dada. 'Father and baby'—and the baby is inside Dada's car.

" 'Sister. Sister and baby. Brother. Brother and baby.' We don't have any brothers and sisters, do we?

" 'Grandmother'—Grandma. 'Grandfather'—Grandpa. That's like our grandpa Mario. Grandpa and baby.

"Baby!

"Yeah—baby.

"Where's the babies? Show me the babies.

"Babies!

"Yeah!"

Rachel listened to this book many times during her first year of life, and one can imagine the complicated process that took place as the words emerged from her world of sound. Marie Ellen holds conversations with Rachel, answering for her daughter as the questions are asked. As she reads the words in the book and shares the pictures on each page, she is giving meaning to Rachel. "Grandfather" is changed to "Grandpa," and Rachel is told that the grandpa in the picture is like her grandpa Mario. In another reading of the book, when Rachel is several months older, she is told that the grandpa in the book smokes a pipe like her grandpa Mario. It is in this way that Marie Ellen weaves a world around the pages of the books as she gives Rachel the words that she will eventually speak. Interestingly, we can also see this process in action if we look at the recurring theme of puppies in Rachel's books. Earlier we saw how Rachel first met the word "puppy" in the book *I Am a Puppy.* When she was seventeen months old, Larry, her father, read a book to her in which a boy meets a puppy as he is walking home. Rachel supplied the word "puppy" as her dad read the story.

Once children become familiar with the words of their favorite books, it becomes fun to play. Inventing new words becomes a legitimate enterprise. When James was almost three, he liked to share a book about trucks and cars with his dad. In one of the pictures was a big red double-decker bus. "Double" was too much for James, so he made up his own word, "duggle." He used the word to play with his Dad, as we can see in the following exchange.

James points.

"Mmmm," ponders his dad. "What's that?"

"Duggle-decker bus," James tells him, enjoying the sound of the words.

"That's a double-decker bus?" his dad plays. "No!" he says.

"This decker bus," James says, pointing at another vehicle.

"No," laughs his dad.

"This duggle bus," giggles James.

"That's a double-decker bus?" grins his Dad. "No!"

James chuckles. "This duggle bus," he says, pointing at the bus.

"Yes," says his dad, laughing with James.

Sarah, whom we've met several times, is also experimenting with words, coming up with new sounds and sometimes new meanings. In a story about a cricket, Sarah rhymed "cricket" with "pigget." Sarah is at a different stage from James. She is learning to read in the traditional sense, and her interest in words is heightened by the task that she is facing. She is beginning to match what she hears with what she sees on the printed page.

Earlier in this chapter we observed her as she read the book *Dear Zoo*. It took time and patience to figure out some of the words, but Sarah was familiar with the text and willing to try. We could listen and watch as her efforts revealed her developing awareness of the words that made up the story. This is an important step in relating to print, since it is only when dealing with print that we need to separate words with spaces. Another way in which Sarah is revealing her new awareness of the concept of word-ness happens when she is listening to new stories, stops her mom, and asks her to show her where it says a particular word that tickles her interest.

While Sarah is searching for words on the page, other word-related things are happening. Cullen sometimes stops if she thinks a word in a story might be new to Sarah. In the story *Chester Cricket's Pigeon Ride* there is a line that speaks of Chester the cricket sunning himself on a stump in the country. Cullen wonders if Sarah understands what "stump" means. She is concerned that the pen-and-ink drawing of the stump is too detailed for Sarah to appreciate that it is a tree stump on which Chester is sunbathing.

"Do you see the stump in this picture, Sarah?"

"This?" Sarah points at the stump in the picture.

"Mmm-mmm," responds her mother. "Where would he sun himself, do you think?"

"In the sun," is Sarah's straightforward answer.

Cullen says, "Right," and then adds a ponderous "Mmm" as she thinks about Sarah's response. Then she pursues her question, "What is a stump, Sarah?"

"A stump?" Sarah asks. "Like this?"

Cullen still wonders if Sarah knows that the stump is the remainder of a tree and so she continues, "Well, what is a stump?"

Sarah answers her mom, "The tree was starting to grow and then somebody says, 'I want to find things to chop,' and he chops the tree."

Cullen goes on, "And what is left?"

Sarah says, "A stump!"

Cullen agrees and says, "And that's where Chester Cricket used to have to sun."

Later in the story Chester's stump is likened to an observation platform for stargazing, but by the time this comes along Sarah is well equipped to understand how that could be. With a little help from her mother and Jessica, her older sister, she works out the meaning of "observation platform" and she understands how Chester could use his stump for stargazing as well as sunbathing.

"Baby," "duggle-bus," "stump," and "observation platform" are words and variations on words that Rachel, James, and Sarah have met sharing stories with their families. They are a part of the endless stream of words and meanings that will help them as they learn to read and write. By listening to them, observing them at work, and talking with them we can watch as they gain an understanding of the many words that they meet and as they express their competence at language learning.

Family storybook reading provides children with the opportunity to hear a variety of language patterns that are not usually a part of everyday speech.

Without doubt the richness of the language that children use is greatly affected by the richness of the language that they hear. If we focus upon just one child, we can begin to appreciate the richness and variety of the language to which all young children are exposed when parents read stories to them.

Among the books that Rachel listened to over and over again and binged on is *Goodnight Moon*. Marie Ellen and Larry began reading the story to her when she was a baby. Rachel would listen quietly. During one reading, Larry speaks to Rachel about the poetic quality of the story and he tells her that if the woman who wrote the story never wrote anything else in her lifetime she would still have achieved something very special. Both parents loved reading the story to Rachel, so it was hardly surprising that she fell in love with the book. Marie Ellen calls *Goodnight Moon* a "breakthrough book," as it was the first book that Rachel was "incredibly enchanted" by. Marie Ellen explains, "There was something in that book, it's a soothing book, a beautiful book that sets up a tremendous sense of security."

Listen to the words of the story that Rachel loves and hear the patterns of language that Margaret Wise Brown offers to young children:

In the great green room
There was a telephone
And a red balloon
And a picture of—

The cow jumping over the moon
And there were three little bears sitting on chairs

And two little kittens
And a pair of mittens
And a little toyhouse
And a young mouse

And a comb and a brush and a bowl full of mush
And a quiet old lady who was whispering "hush"

Goodnight room
Goodnight moon

And so it continues right to the last lines:

Goodnight stars
Goodnight air
Goodnight noises everywhere

When Rachel was seventeen months old and the lullaby of *Goodnight Moon* was one of her favorite books, she also listened to the practical language of *A Bag Full of Pup* and the delightfully frightening story *Where the Wild Things Are*. Again, listen to the

patterns of language that this Maurice Sendak tale brings to young children. At the beginning of the story Max is sent to his room without supper:

> *That very night in Max's room a forest grew*
> *and grew—*
> *and grew until his ceiling hung with vines*
> *and the walls became the world all around*
> *and an ocean tumbled by with a private boat for Max*
> *and he sailed off through night and day*
> *and in and out of weeks*
> *and almost over a year*
> *to where the wild things are.*

Later in the book come the lines that children love to hear:

> *The wild things roared their terrible roars and gnashed their terrible teeth*
> *and rolled their terrible eyes and showed their terrible claws*
> *but Max stepped into his private boat and waved goodbye*

Now let's add another dimension to the variety of language patterns to which Rachel is exposed and look at her love of nursery rhymes, and of one nursery rhyme in particular. One evening after *Goodnight Moon* and *Where the Wild Things Are*, Rachel wants to listen to nursery rhymes. She gives her mom her book of Mother Goose rhymes and listens while Marie Ellen reads. When they reach "I Had a Little Hen," Rachel starts saying another of the rhymes that is in the book.

" 'Humpdy Dumpdy,' " Rachel begins. " 'Humpdy Dumpdy had fall. Humpdy Dumpdy had fall.' "

Marie Ellen stops reading and sounds both surprised and happy to hear Rachel saying the nursery rhyme. "Very good! That's 'Humpty Dumpty.' Shall we do 'Humpty Dumpty'? Good for you, Rachel!"

"Humpdy Dumpdy," Rachel says.

Marie Ellen turns to the index and looks for the nursery rhyme. "Let's see," she says, and then she adds another "Very good" to Rachel. "O.K. Page forty," she tells Rachel as she looks for the page. "Oh! Who's that?"

"Humpdy Dumpdy."

" 'Humpty Dumpty sat on a . . . ,' " Marie Ellen stops.

"Wall," says Rachel.

" 'Humpty Dumpty had a great . . .' "

"Fall."

50

*How Will Fam-
ily Storybook
Sharing Help
My Child to
Read and
Write?*

"Good," Marie Ellen tells Rachel. " 'All the king's . . .' "

"Horses."

" 'And all the king's . . .' "

"Men."

" 'Couldn't put . . .' "

"Humpdy gether."

"Together," Marie Ellen says, pleased with Rachel.

"Together," repeats Rachel.

" 'Again.' "

"Again," Rachel adds.

"Very good!" says her mom.

Rachel listens, adds words that she remembers from prior readings, and copies new words that her mom says. She is learning to use language patterns that are outside of the language that she hears spoken in her everyday life.

The important point to be made here is that Rachel, like all children who are read to, is more apt to be sensitive to the power of language and the seemingly endless possibilities for its use. This kind of sensitivity is a tremendous asset to bring to the task of learning to read and write.

Often you can observe children as they repeat patterns that they have been introduced to through books. Such children are experimenting with the shapes and patterns of language. They are trying out their own language power to see what they can create.

S haring storybooks with young children encourages them to engage in language play that is often centered on the sounds of language.

Just as the patterns of language are known to captivate children's imaginations, the sounds within these patterns are also apt to delight the ears and tickle the tongues of even the very youngest child. For example, when we were looking at the patterns of language, we saw how Humpty Dumpty had delighted Rachel, and we also saw how she liked to join her mother in saying the rhyme. Think about some of the other rhymes that Rachel loves and that have a universal appeal for all children who listen to them:

Pat-a-cake, pat-a-cake,
Baker's man!
So I do, master,
As fast as I can.

Pat it, and prick it,
And mark it with T,
Put it in the oven
For Tommy and me.

Hey, diddle, diddle!
The cat and the fiddle,
The cow jumped over the moon;
The little dog laughed
To see such sport,
And the dish ran away with the spoon.

Children do not seek to make sense of these nursery rhymes, for part of the magic is the sounds that they hear as the rhymes are read or sung to them over and over again. They are captivated by the melody that they hear. When children hear these rhymes it isn't long before they begin to chime in with the rhyming words at the end of each line. Soon entire lines and verses are chanted by heart as children delight in the unusual sounds of the language.

There are many opportunities for such experiences in the books that children share with their parents. James loved the rhyme in *Pierre* by Maurice Sendak. It was one of the books that he binged on. When he was two and three he would sit on the floor with the book on his lap, turning the pages and talking the story. Then, every so often he would use the words of the text as he shouted aloud, "I don't care! I don't care!"

Children absorbed in the sounds of language sometimes play with speech in their own made-up songs. One young boy we know made up rhymes of sounds that he would chant for hours in his bed or on long car rides. The sounds resembled words, but they had no meaning. Nevertheless, he would tell himself a story as he chanted on and on into sleep. Such "epic poets" are not unusual, and parents can often observe their children playing in similar ways with sound. Sometimes it is the sound of individual words that delight them. Think of James and his "duggle bus" and Sarah experimenting with "cricket" and "piget." At other times it is the repetition of a single sound, perhaps an initial consonant, as in the story *Diamond Dee and the Dreadful*

Dragon, which Debbie and Kathy loved having their mother read to them. It begins, "Dozens of years ago in a drafty castle Duke David of Dundeedle did dwell."

Such sensitivity to the sounds of language goes hand in hand with children's awareness that symbols represent meaning. Obviously, such ideas take time and experience to develop. But what begins as a subtle growing awareness of sounds matures slowly into an explicit recognition that sounds and symbols are related. In the next chapter we will expand upon this notion and look at the ways in which children begin to write as well as read.

Most parents are very much aware of the great emphasis that is placed upon sound–symbol relationships when young children are learning to read and spell. In today's schools, it is customary to teach these relationships in the earliest grades. Children who have an opportunity to begin to make these connections through many and varied language experiences are indeed fortunate. They can begin to unlock the system for themselves, and that is much better than being force-fed a series of abstract and often inconsistent rules.

S haring books with children fosters their ability to listen, which is an essential requirement for learning, both in and out of school.

Listening is closely related to reading, and both involve high-level thinking. Children learn to make meaning from the sounds that they hear. As they grow, they learn to obtain information about the world and relate that information to what they already know. If we review this chapter and examine why story reading helps young children as they learn to read and write, we will find that learning to listen is an essential component of each reason that we have given. Developing a sense of story, learning about words, discovering patterns of language, and enjoying the sounds of language all depend upon learning to listen.

Unfortunately, too often the development of listening skills is thought to be synonymous with "paying attention." The myth is that the "good" listener sits quietly, does not interrupt the reader, enjoys every book equally well, and is properly grateful for the experience. Clearly, this is not so. There are children who listen quietly, but there are also children, such as Matthew and Nan, who love books and enjoy family storybook reading and yet play while they are listening.

When Nan was two and three it was not unusual for her to

play while her mother read to her older sisters. Kate, her mother, would include her, drawing her into the books that they shared. "Here, Nan. Sit up here," she would say. "What's this? What's this, Nan?" And when Nan said, "Bye-bye," and moved off across the room, her mom said, "No, Nan. Come on back." Nan was learning to listen; and although her mother worked to engage her interest in the story, she did not make Nan sit still or punish her in any way.

Reading stories is a family affair. It is for this reason that the information covered in the previous chapter is so important. Reading stories is not an activity added to the family agenda specifically to teach reading. Rather, books become a part of the very fabric of family life.

At a professional meeting at which we were talking about family storybook reading, we were asked why a mother would try to read a book to her children when the oldest was in elementary school and the youngest just learning to talk. We answered the question, but later we posed the same question to a mother who often read stories to her oldest child and her youngest child. Her response was quick and straightforward. "They are both members of my family," she said. "How could I read to one and not the other?"

Learning to listen is a part of the dynamic role that family storybook reading plays in the lives of young children. It is all right for the two-year-old to play while the seven-year-old sits. Both may be listening and enjoying the story in their own way. Remember Sarah and what she said when she was asked about the photos of Matthew that were taken when their mother was reading to them. "What's Matthew doing?" we asked. "He's listening to the story," she said. The fact that Matthew was playing with his toys did not bother Sarah. Matthew loves books and is learning to listen even though he is busy doing things.

Very often, children are listening attentively when it appears that they are not. Don't wait for children to sit still before you start to read. The children who wander around the room, draw with crayons, or build with blocks may well be the ones who can recount every aspect of the story. And sometimes they are the ones who are upset when a word is missed or a sentence changed when the story is read just one more time. Listening can take place well before children learn to sit still and "pay attention" in the way that is often expected of them in school.

4 WHAT CAN I DO TO HELP MY CHILD LEARN MORE ABOUT WRITTEN LANGUAGE WHILE WE ARE SHARING BOOKS?

In chapter 2 we talked about the ways in which family storybook reading grows quietly in the home, and we emphasized that it is not an activity added to the family agenda specifically to teach young children to read and write. On the contrary, as we tried to show in chapter 3, it is precisely because storybook reading is such a natural part of the daily life of the family that it is so beneficial to the young reader. Sharing a story doesn't have to become a lesson for it to help young children to learn to read and write. This makes our task more difficult, for the question that we have posed for this chapter is "What can I do to help my child learn more about written language while we are sharing books?" From the position that we have taken thus far, clearly we do not wish to present you with a list of "things to do" during storybook reading. Fortunately, we have the families that we have written about to learn from as we try to answer the question. With their help, we would like to suggest ways in which you can create supportive learning environments for your children that will encourage language learning and help them learn to read and write.

Let's begin by taking another look at the three storybook occasions that we used to introduce the previous chapters.

In the first excerpt, Cullen has just read one of Sarah's books, and she is now reading a book that belongs to Matthew, *My Shirt Is White*, by Dick Bruna.

"Where are the red socks, Matthew?"

"Where the socks?" asks Matthew, playing the game.

Cullen plays with him: "Where are the red socks?"

Matthew says his own words for "I don't know," and turns two pages.

58

*What Can I Do
to Help My
Child Learn
More About
Written Lan-
guage While
We Are Shar-
ing Books?*

Cullen reads, " 'My dress is red,' " and then she adds, "Here, turn the page." Matthew turns. " 'My ribbons are yellow,' " reads his mom, and then she asks, "These the yellow ribbons, Matthew?"

"Yes," says Sarah.

"Yes," agrees Matthew. He makes the sound for yellow.

Sarah speaks to Matthew, as if reading to him. "Here are what we see," she says, using a turn of phrase that she thinks is appropriate for a two-year-old who is sharing a book with his mother and sister.

Matthew turns the page. " 'My shoes are black,' " reads Cullen. Then she asks, "Where're the black shoes, Matthew?"

"Here shoes," says Matthew.

"I see shoes," agrees Cullen, playing the game.

"And socks," adds Matthew.

"Oh, and socks too," agrees Cullen.

"And sock too," repeats Matthew, enjoying the to-and-fro of the conversation with his mom.

In the second excerpt, it is bedtime and Marie Ellen and Rachel have been reading stories. Another book is finished, and Marie Ellen asks her daughter, "What next?"

Rachel climbs down off the bed to look for another book, and as she searches she talks to her Mom. "I want, um. . . . How's that?" she says, holding up a book for her mother to see.

Marie Ellen reads the title: *One Dark Night.* Oh boy," she says encouragingly.

"No. No," responds Rachel.

"No?" her mother questions.

"No," says Rachel with finality. She goes back to her looking.

In the third excerpt, James is sick, and he is playing his favorite game with his mother, Donna. He is looking for the mouse in the pictures of *Goodnight Moon*.

James has just turned the page to a new picture of the red and green room, and he studies it carefully. "Where?" he asks his mom as he looks for the mouse. "Where, Mom?"

Donna waits a moment. "Do you want me to give you a hint?" she says.

James takes a breath, thrusts out his hand, and points. He has found the mouse.

Donna laughs, "You found him!"

James laughs with his mother and turns the page. There in front of him are two black-and-white pictures of things that appear in the red and green room. "Goodnight," James says, and then, using the words of the text, he "reads" the next line, " 'Goodnight kittens.' "

Donna reads it after him: " 'Goodnight kittens.' "

James looks at the next page and "reads" the next line of the text. " 'Goodnight mittens,' " he says.

"Goodnight," Donna adds.

When these short pieces are gathered together, what is most striking is the active participation of the children. Matthew, Rachel, and James are not passive recipients of the words in the books. Instead, they are story builders who work out what the story is about, they are decision makers who choose the books to be shared, and they are the inventors of games to play with their parents. They are engaged in the pleasure of the moment and are not planning for some future event. Learning to read is not high on their agenda, even though they have been involved in that complicated process from the very first time that a book was opened and a story shared. It would seem from our discussions with parents that it is all this that makes sharing books so enjoyable. Even parents who haven't had any experience of reading stories with young children, and those who are nervous about reading aloud to children, soon find that it is the children themselves who lead the way and make the sharing easy. In a very short time, parents learn to build upon the experiences of their children, expanding their everyday world as they help them gain new skills.

Parents can help their children think and talk about the stories that they read.

Many of the books that parents and children share have pictures on every page. Children love to pore over the pictures to find the story in the brightly colored pages. Details can be talked about. For a very young child, like Matthew, such things as white shirts and red socks are important. Reading Dick Bruna's book gives Matthew the opportunity to link the white shirt in the book with the one that he wears. And even if his socks are not red, he learns that they are still the same things and that they have the same name. Even when children are this young, parents can

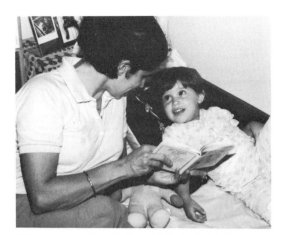

provide the opportunity for them to interpret the pictures and to think critically and imaginatively.

In the story-reading excerpts presented throughout this book, we have seen how parents who engage their children in storybook reading help them find their own ways of sharing so that they can make the stories their own. Marie Ellen's willingness to let Rachel choose books and Donna's readiness to play the game of looking for the mouse with James are both important ways in which they are helping their children to think and talk about books. Very often it just takes a question—"Where are the red socks, Matthew?" "What next?" "Do you want me to give you a hint?"—and the child is ready to think and talk about the story.

Perhaps the most annoying, yet paradoxically sometimes the most pleasurable, thing that happens when children listen to stories is that they want to hear the same story over and over again. We have often heard parents say that they have read one book every night for a month and they wish they could read something else. Courage! Just think what is happening when a child becomes so involved with a single book. Sometimes it is only after a book has been shared on a number of occasions that questions emerge and many understandings develop.

Even when children are very young, each sharing adds to their world. In chapter 3, we made this point when we shared several of the readings that Rachel listened to of *I Am a Puppy*. Marie Ellen read "I hate baths," and then she talked to Rachel about her own bath: "Rachel likes her bath." In a later reading, she talks about Bruno taking off his collar and Rachel taking off her clothes when they get ready for a bath. Little bits of stories are different every time. Then, when the stories are so familiar that parents and children know them by heart, new variations can be played, and "reading stories silly" becomes a favorite game as the words of the book are changed into outrageous dialogues that only the child and the parent can fully understand. Still, the children are learning. Such play gives them the opportunity to think critically and imaginatively as they learn to interpret the pictures and the text, inventing new variations that become stories upon stories.

Thus, as children learn to think and talk about stories, they increase their awareness of what makes a story. Story language such as "Once upon a time" begins to creep into their own telling of the tales that they read in books, and as they grow, such language becomes a part of the repertoire of words that they will use in the stories that they write.

Parents can provide their children with informal ways of learning about print while they are sharing stories.

The talk that surrounds the words and pictures in books inevitably turns to questions about print. Sometimes this happens when children are quite young. When Sarah was in kindergarten she would often find a particular word or phrase enticing, and she would ask her mother to find the word or words for her. Matthew, who was then three, would watch this process and would also want to see the word that had interested Sarah. Then, when telling himself a story he would point to the words in the book that he was reading. Usually, children begin by recognizing that it is the squiggles on the page that tell the reader what to say. It is in this way that the important idea that *print carries meaning* begins to emerge. Gradually, as children grow older, questions about words and letters are asked. Children begin to see that similar shapes and forms appear over and over again. Talking about written language becomes a natural part of story sharing, but again we want to emphasize that it needn't be forced. Children are curious and ask questions, and parents try to answer. Talking about how books are held, how pages are turned, what the words say, and how words come in straight lines all takes place at the appropriate time.

Letters themselves eventually become a source of great interest, and children like to talk about them, write them, and learn them. Usually, it is the four- or five-year-old who finds letters so intriguing. At this age name writing becomes important, and letters in books become doubly significant. Sometimes children will use the few letters they know to write stories that they tell. Scribbles on a page can be a story that is "written" as children bring everything that they know about language to the act of creating a story for themselves. At such times, they are demonstrating that they have some understanding that symbols represent meaning, and that what is conveyed through written symbols can be read both by themselves and by others. They might also know that the same symbols are used over and over again, that letters and words have special patterns, and that the sounds in words are represented by letters. None of this should be taught directly to the young child. Unless the child *wants* the information, it has no meaning. As with all the things we would teach young children, it is hard to wait for the child, and parents often feel an urgent need to sit down and teach their children directly about letters and words, symbols and sounds. Resist. Share books and be ready to talk about language. The rest will follow in good time.

Parents can help their children learn what readers and writers do.

Learning that the story being read was once a thought that someone wished to share is difficult for young children. It is hard for them to imagine that the words and pictures that appear on a page actually started in someone's imagination. Indeed, the long process involved from the time that the idea was conceived and written to the completion of the published work is difficult for many adults to comprehend.

Sometimes parents and children work it out together. One day, when Cullen was reading *Chester Cricket's Pigeon Ride*, Sarah asked her about the illustrations. "He does good drawings," she said. Then Sarah pointed to the fine line drawings and asked her mother who made them. Cullen tells her that they were made by Garth Williams. "With crayons?" questions Sarah. Cullen asks her what she thinks and Sarah asks another question, "Did he copy with a machine?" "No," Cullen says, "I think he probably drew them himself and the machine reproduced them in the book." Jessica joins in the conversation and tells Sarah that she thinks the pictures were made with a pen and she adds, "A special kind of pen." "Pen and ink and a special machine," says Sarah. "And then a special machine," Cullen says as she gets ready to read the story.

The fundamental idea that children need to know is that what people think about and talk about can be written down and shared by others. How easy it would be if we could just sit them down and tell them that. But again, it would have no meaning. Young children learn of such things as the need arises. Learning about authorship occurs when they themselves begin to write stories for themselves. Then all the talk that takes place during storybook reading about the title of the book and the author begins to have personal significance. Even "The End" becomes important.

The important thing to remember is that what children learn from one language experience they use and develop in other language experiences. What they learn through book sharing they can use in writing, and what they learn through experimenting with writing they can use as the basis for understanding about print when reading. Creating an environment in which books can be shared and stories written provides children with the opportunity to develop understanding of what it means to be an author as well as what it means to be a reader. The two go hand in hand and can be talked about as questions are asked and answers given.

Parents can provide opportunities for their children to view books as sources of pleasure and information.

One of the recurring themes throughout this book has been that family storybook reading provides children with almost limitless opportunities for learning the whys and wherefores of everyday life. The activity gives families a framework for talking about the world in which we live. In addition, it is one of the ways in which parents can show their enjoyment of learning through the discoveries that they share with their children.

At the beginning of this book we wrote about Cindy, a single mother, and her five adopted children. Cindy shared a Pearl Buck story, *Matthew, Mark, Luke and John*, with her children, and we noted the special kind of sharing that took place as Christopher learned for the first time of the plight of children whose early years were so like those of his sisters and brother. The book enabled Chris to make connections between the lives of Emilie, Ben, and Caroline and the lives of the children in the story. It provided him with new ways of seeing, and it gave his family a chance to come together in ways that may have been difficult if it were not for the book.

Moves, visits to hospitals, new babies, and the death of a grandparent are all emotional events in the lives of young children that can be understood a little better through the warmth and comfort of sharing a well-chosen book. Sometimes such books provide the parent with ways of talking about sensitive issues that have eluded other explanation. For some parents human sexuality is almost impossible to talk about. One young boy we know rushed downstairs after a long discussion with his father and announced, "We need more books with diagrams! Dad's having trouble!" Fortunately for the boy and his father, they were used to "looking things up." The everyday routine of using books as a source of information got them through a tricky moment.

However, as we've emphasized before, books also provide opportunities for sharing information about less sensitive issues. Children are continuously gathering information as they share stories with family members. Matthew and Rachel had many encounters with the world through the pages of their books, and sometimes those encounters took place before they had similar real-life experiences. For example, many animals are introduced this way. Lions and tigers might appear in pictures in storybooks and so might elephants such as Babar, but it is only after a visit to a zoo or a circus that children get to see such animals in real life. Real-life experiences can also lead back into things learned in books. "Like in my book," is a favorite comment of our two-year-old friend Eliza, as she makes connections between her everyday life and the stories that she reads with her mother and father.

Sometimes the confusing contraptions that are met in everyday life can be explained through a story. Parents can explain in greater detail the reasons why and the functions of whatever it is that is puzzling or confusing the young child. It is easy to

see that a parent may not even be aware of some muddles and misconceptions until talking with the child during the sharing of a story. At other times it is the representation in the book that is confusing, leading to a discussion of real-life happenings. Remember Karen reading to Christina and their discussion about elevators and cameras in chapter 1?

The point is that books are a constant source of pleasure and information. They almost always provide opportunities for sharing everyday views of the world, and sometimes they provide parents with opportunities for sharing information about fragile and sensitive issues.

Another way for children to learn the value of books, one that is of inestimable value, is for them to see the adults in their lives using books as sources of pleasure and information. Reading newspapers, "curling up with a good book," and looking up a particular recipe in a cookbook all carry messages for young children. When children see an adult reading books about different breeds of dogs when choosing a new puppy or reading a bus schedule before traveling at a new time or to a new place, they see print in action. Very often such occasions provide parents with opportunities not only for demonstrating the uses of print, but also for sharing it with the child.

As children grow, they too should have opportunities to use books as resources for particular kinds of information. Cookbooks for children abound, and they provide an everyday example of a specialized text that can be used for information and pleasure. Fortunately, a wide variety of children's books are available on every conceivable topic a child might ask about or be interested in. Planting gardens, understanding the changes in the weather, and learning about ancient dinosaurs are all topics easy to explore through books. Needless to say, they are also topics that can be shared.

Parents can help their children by providing them with opportunities to extend and expand upon the pleasures of book sharing.

Besides books, one of the best gifts a young child can receive is a thick pad of plain paper and a box of crayons or felt pens. Don't wait for children to grow. It is in those first smudged lines on paper that young children begin to learn to write, and when children begin to talk about their scribbles they are showing that they understand that the marks they are making mean something. This is one of the ways in which they learn that thoughts and ideas can be written down and communicated with others. Here again we want to emphasize the connection between reading and writing. What children learn from one language experience can be used and developed in other language experiences.

This is certainly true when young children make books. Parents have often talked to us about the books that their children make. We are fascinated by this aspect of literacy development, but we had never had the opportunity to observe children as they make books in family settings. We decided to spend some time making books with some young children in one of our homes and, although we appreciate that making books in our kitchen is not the same as making books in family settings, we do feel that observing the children gave us some insights that we would like to share.

The children were in their second semester of kindergarten, and none of them were in programs that provided them with much opportunity to write on their own. Writing was a workbook page or something copied from a chalkboard. All we did was to provide them with opportunities to make books. A kitchen table, all kinds of paper, some crayons and markers, and some paints were all that was needed.

"You write the story," they said when we began, and that is exactly what we did. We wrote down the words as they made up the story together. The children crowded around and talked with one another. They talked quickly, building upon the ideas and watching as the words were written down. They moved back and forth among the pages, tossing ideas from one to another as together they worked out what the story would say. Phrases and words were patiently repeated when the writing could not keep up with the rapid development of the story, until there was an almost continuous replay superimposed upon the newly created story.

After that first visit to our kitchen the children wrote stories for themselves, even though they asked for words to be written down for them to copy and for words to be spelled out loud. Watching them taught us much about their knowledge of books and stories. They all began writing on the first page, and the "Once upon a time" that began some of the books told us that they knew something about the language of stories. One page followed another in an orderly fashion, but they also moved back and forth as they developed their ideas. They wanted to hear what they had written and would listen and think for a while before beginning a new page. Their thoughts were connected; they did not just write a disconnected commentary on the content of each page. Words tumbled into one another as they wrote and some things were crossed out, but the stories made sense. The children were authors, writing for themselves.

As they became more comfortable about writing in our kitchen, the children began to explore other ways in which they could find the words that they needed. Some of the words they had written in their first books were found and copied as they wanted them. "Eggs" and "birds" were copied in this way. During an early visit, one of the children finished a story and asked for "The end" to be written down on a piece of paper. Another child had already written it, and she showed the others where to find "The end" on the last page of the first book that they had made.

Then came the precious moment when, one by one, the children felt confident enough to write their own words, and their words became their own inventions. One child drew a rainbow with markers and crayons, and under the picture she wrote "RBY":

Another child drew a family of bunnies and wrote "Bez" on the page. Another drew a bird and wrote "BrD."

70

*What Can I Do
to Help My
Child Learn
More About
Written Lan-
guage While
We Are Shar-
ing Books?*

That day, when the children were picked up, one child told
her mother, "I wrote a word today." For the child it was an
important occasion. The word belonged to her. She had written
it herself. She still asked for some words to be written down and
she still copied words that she had written in previous stories,
but her ways of writing words were expanding, and she could
invent her own spelling and use the words that she made in the
stories that she wrote.

Making books can be infectious. At home the children worked
on their own constructions. Their parents, knowing of our interest, saved many of these books for us to see. There was a
math book in which was written, "These problems are for you
to figure out."

$$1+1=$$
$$5+5=$$
$$6+6=$$
$$7+7=$$
$$5+5=$$
$$6+6=$$
$$7+7=$$
$$8+8=$$
$$9+9=$$
$$10+10=$$

These Prodlems
are for You Ta figure out

There was a picture book inside of which was written "Rainbows
are beautiful,"

71
*What Can I Do
to Help My
Child Learn
More About
Written Lan-
guage While
We Are Shar-
ing Books?*

a little book with the names of family members inside,

an ABC book tied up with red ribbon,

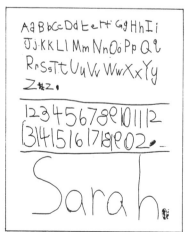

and a book on a father's notepaper in which was written, "This book was fun to make."

Even one three-year-old joined in the fun and made a book like his sister's. He got his mother to write the words "Color Book" on the cover and inside he dictated "Color books are everywhere that melt into spring." On the next page he asked his mom to write "Red, yellow, blue, orange, green, and brown." This she did, matching the names of the colors to the colors of the pens that she used. On the last page he asked her to write "The end."

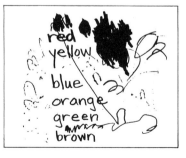

As time went by and the children made more books, their stories became more complex. One storybook had "Book" and "Daddy" written on the cover, and inside was the following story, written with some requested "how-do-you-spell" help from Mom:

I had a bear
his name was Fred
I was born with the bear
He was my favorite Bear
Then a bear came
he was He was new
Then I remember my old Bear
then I love both of them.

Paper and markers, staples and glue. Nothing fancy, just a few basic materials and a little imagination are all that are needed for books to be made. Odd pieces of cardboard can become beautiful covers, and a few old pipe cleaners can become an ingenious way to hold a book together.

Some children prefer to write their stories with little or no help. Others may wish to copy the words that they have dictated to you. In either case, don't worry about their spelling or about whether they write on the lines of the paper. It's the ideas that count. Whole stories (as well as the desire to write) may be lost when children are made to feel that making the letters rest on the lines or spelling the words correctly is more important than getting their ideas down in print. We wouldn't think of expecting babies to begin to talk by pronouncing every word as an adult would pronounce it. We are much too interested in what they are saying to stifle their talk with speech lessons. Attempting to communicate, share ideas, and talk with one another is all that we care about. We know that young children need time to develop in an atmosphere where they can take risks in what they say without being held responsible for talking like adults.

The same thing is true when children learn to write. Their scribbles mean something. The lines they draw on paper can be a letter to a friend, a shopping list to take to the store, or a story to read with their family or friends. In fact, observing your children as they write words for themselves is another valuable way to discover what they know about language. The children who wrote "Bez" for bunnies and "BrD" for bird under their pictures were demonstrating that they know there are many ways to represent their ideas. They talk, draw pictures, and write stories. They showed us that they are aware that words are usually formed by clustering groups of letters together. They also showed us that they know a great deal about the sounds of their language and the letters that stand for those sounds; they even managed to put the letters in the order in which the sounds occur. When we look positively at the children's invented spelling from the standpoint of what it reveals, we can value it as evidence of their growing knowledge about language rather than characterize it simply as groups of misspelled words.

Parents can make family storybooks with their children.

The most important story that a family has to share is its own. Everyday events can be written down in diaries and journals. Even very young children like to record what happens to them during the day. Picture stories with a few dictated words that are written down by Dad or Mom can grow into books that can be shared in the months to come. One grandfather that we met told us about the book that he had given his grandson. They lived in a remote part of Canada, and a light aircraft was their link to other places. The four-year-old often flew in his grandfather's small plane, and he kept a flight book in which his grandfather wrote the distances that they'd travelled and the places that they'd been. The little boy treasured his book. He liked to study the record of the journeys that he had made.

Flying is a part of one young child's life, just as cats are a part of another child's life. Ellen's mother, Anne, makes quilts, pillows, and wall hangings and sells them in the village where they live. Her favorite motifs are of cats—richly embroidered cats, reclining cats, and long, lean cats. Many of the designs seem to come from the four cats that share Ellen's home. They curl up in boxes of materials and embroidery silks, stalk across tables, and purr when Ellen, who is in kindergarten, picks them up. It is small wonder that Ellen made a book entitled *Cats*. The book consists of three small pages stuck together with some masking tape. On the cover Ellen has written the title and underneath, the name of the author. On the first page she has written "Mommy cat with all her kittens," on the next page, "Just a happy cat," and on the next, "Just a alley cat." A "Scottish Cat" comes next. On the back of the book is "Just a regular cat." Anne said that Ellen has made books for a long time and that she used to ask Anne to write the words down so that she could copy them. Now she asks her mother to spell the words for her.

After Ellen had given us her book of cats she wondered if she should have kept it for herself. Her mom suggested that she make another book, and that is exactly what Ellen did. A few weeks later Anne showed it to us. In one of the pictures Ollie, Ellen's cat, is thinking about Ellen pouring milk. In another, Ollie is watching the rain and thinking, "Meow." Anne explained, "When Ellen was little I would always say to her, 'The cats are saying this,' or 'The cats are saying that.' And after a while, she would look at them and say to me, 'What are the cats saying?' And I would have to tell her." Anne smiled at this point and added, "Now she knows!"

On the third page of Ellen's book she has written, "Mommy trying to work with help." Anne looked at the smiling picture of herself and said that she liked the smiling faces in the book and the little details in the pictures, such as the scissors that she is holding in this particular picture. She looked at the cats curled up on the bundles of fabric and said, "I ordinarily have at least one or two cats in the sewing room." She pointed to a pile of fabric that had two cats curled up on top. "Usually there is an argument going on in the pile of fabric over who's going to have the choice spot under the light. That's very warm. And then there's a cat under the table and there's always a cat on the box. They all have their special spots." Ellen came over and looked at the picture. She pointed to the work table and explained, "Rosemary always is behind the table under there."

In the next picture Ollie is dreaming and purring. Anne explains, "He's dreaming of Ellen pouring milk and Dad building a cat house," and then she laughed. "He knows he's the prince," she says.

Picture stories with a few dictated words truly can become family books to be shared in the months and years to come.

Special books can be made for special occasions. Birthday cards can be collected in a scrapbook to keep, and summer photos can

77

*What Can I Do
to Help My
Child Learn
More About
Written Lan-
guage While
We Are Shar-
ing Books?*

be put in albums to be talked about on snowy days. The opportunities are limitless. When Marie Ellen and Larry won a trip to
Africa in a raffle they took lots of photos. Back home they made
a book for Rachel who had stayed home with her grandparents.
They filled the pages with the places that they'd stayed and the
wildlife that they'd seen. The album became known as *Rachel's
Book*, and she has spent many happy hours poring over the
pictures with her mother and father.

Rachel's book served a special purpose, as it helped Marie
Ellen and Larry share with her the time when they were far
away. Such books can often be made to fulfill special needs.
Cindy's little girl, Alison, has a book to help her learn to talk.
Alison is three and has cerebral palsy. Her book is called *Alison's
Book of Family*. On the inside of the front cover it says, "To Al-
ee from Mommy! Happy Talking." On each page is a picture of
someone in her family, and underneath each picture is the person's name. The pages are coated with clear plastic to make them
sturdy and easy to handle. Cindy often shares the book with
Alison and talks to her about the people in the photos. When
Cindy is busy, Alison continues looking at the book on her own,
enjoying the smiling faces of her brothers and sister and the
pages on which she herself appears.

We too have used photographs in books that we have made
with parents and children. We would like to end this chapter by
giving you an idea of how simply these books can be made.

You will need:

1. Wallpaper for the front and back covers.
2. A thin strip of wallpaper to make the spine of the book.
3. Drawing paper for the pages of the book.
4. Scissors.
5. Glue.
6. Staples.
7. A family photo.

Cut the wallpaper into two pieces large enough to be folded
in half so that the inside of the cover is as pretty as the outside.
Each piece should be twice the size of the inside pages.

Decide on the number of pages that the book will have (3 to
6), and make sure that the paper is a little smaller than the
wallpaper when it is folded in half. (The wallpaper is going to
become the front and back cover.)

Put one piece of paper aside. The photograph that you have
chosen will eventually be affixed to this, the last page of the
book.

HOW TO MAKE A BOOK

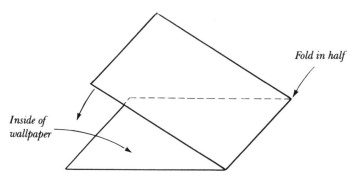

Fold in half

Inside of wallpaper

1. Make the cover. (You need two sheets, a little longer and wider than the inside pages.)

Cut out windows to show the picture

2. Make the pages (as many as you like).

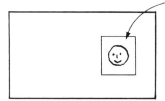

Glue picture in position so that it shows through the windows in the other pages

3. The last page (with picture).

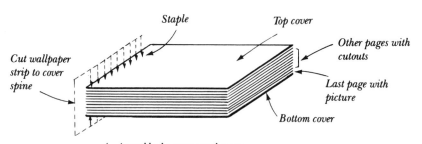

Staple   *Top cover*

Other pages with cutouts

Cut wallpaper strip to cover spine

Last page with picture

Bottom cover

4. Assemble the covers and pages.

Fold the thin strip of wallpaper over the spine to cover the staples and glue it in place.

5. Finish off the spine.

The other pages will need a window cut in them to frame the picture. On each page, mark where you would like the picture to show through. Then, with a sharp pair of scissors, cut out the rectangles of paper.

Place all the pages together and place the picture on the page that you put aside. Position it so that the picture shows right through to the front page, and stick the picture in place with a little glue or tape.

Place the two covers over the back and the front of the pages and staple all the sheets together.

Then take the thin strip that you cut to make the spine of the book and fold it in half. Glue it over the stapled edge of the book to give the book a finished spine.

You can do all this yourself or you can share the cutting and gluing with your child. However you decide to proceed, when the book is finished share the writing with a child.

5 WHERE CAN I FIND GOOD BOOKS TO SHARE?

After looking closely at families and storybook reading we now want to shift our focus to the books themselves. It is somewhat paradoxical that although there are several thousand new books for children published each year, children's books are sometimes hard to find. Inner-city families may find that they are two bus rides away from a store that stocks children's titles. Families living in country locations have to drive many miles to find a bookstore that can provide them with the books that they need. And, very often, families living in suburban locations face similar difficulties. Adult paperbacks usually fill the shelves, and children's books are tucked away in a small space in some distant corner. But however difficult and frustrating it can be, searching for children's books can be both fruitful and rewarding. There are good bookstores to be found, and ingenious parents will find many other ways to fill their homes with books for their children to enjoy. Good books become special treasures that can be listened to today and read tomorrow. Finding them is well worth the effort. Hopefully these thoughts about some of the difficulties and rewards of the search for children's books has whetted your appetite for the question that we now want to pursue as we ask ourselves, "Where can I find good books to share?"

For many adults, the books that are remembered with the greatest affection are those that belonged to them as children and were read over and over again. Children love to own books, to pile them up, to enjoy the colors, and to browse through the pages as they share the stories that will become memories to cherish in later life. It is important for children to have time to enjoy their books in their own way; and, while they certainly need help in learning how to care for books, they need not think of books as something sacred. Children need access to books just as they need access to their dolls and trucks and other important possessions.

Though libraries are an important source of books for children (a fact we stress later in this chapter), investing in books that can be read over and over again through the years as children grow and begin to read them for themselves is crucial. Having books available as one of the many choices of things to do in spare moments is an important part of growing up literate. Even the very youngest members of the family soon come to know the titles that belong to them, and they take great pride in selecting books from their own collection for reading alone and together. It is for this reason that we want to begin our search for storybooks by looking at some of the ways in which parents can begin to build personal collections for their children. However, we want to do this realistically, for many of the parents with whom we have spoken must rely on the convenience of local shopping, and very often they cannot afford to buy expensive books for their children. Luckily, there are other options.

Parents can find many inexpensive and enjoyable books in such unlikely places as the supermarket, the pharmacy, and even the hospital.

Hidden among the workbooks (which we would advise you to ignore) are some storybooks worth buying. Folktales and nursery rhymes are supermarket favorites. *The Three Little Pigs*, *Little Red Riding Hood*, and *Mother Goose* all find their way onto the shelves along with the peanut butter and breakfast cereal. Some of these books deal with the special needs of children, such as the one that we recently bought about a little girl called Amy who is growing up. She is too big for her baby carriage, too big for her playpen, and too big for her baby bathtub, but as we learn on the last page of *When You Were a Baby*, she'll "never, *never* be too big to hug." Another book that we purchased recently is called *The Animal Quiz Book*. Even elementary school children would enjoy the format of this book. At the top of each page is a question ("What is the largest animal in the world?") and at the bottom of the page is the answer ("The Blue Whale. It is bigger than the biggest elephant, and bigger than the biggest dinosaur

that ever lived"). Each of these inexpensive Little Golden Books would make a welcome treat for the young shopper. But just as peanut butter and cereal do not make for a balanced diet, neither do supermarket books.

Department stores also offer many opportunities for parents to buy inexpensive books.

Discount department stores often have a table of children's books that are on sale. Very often there are books priced below a dollar. If you sort through the pile, you can easily find titles that would make welcome additions to any young child's collection. At one discount department store we found a series of Merrigold Press books on sale, six books for a dollar. *Mother Goose*, *The Bremen Town Musicians*, and a book called *Once I had a Monster* were among the books that we purchased for a dollar. We found another *Mother Goose* and an abridged edition of *Puppies Are Like That* published by Happy House. We also found a Whitman Book entitled *Toys for Baby* that was advertised as nontoxic with wipe-clean pages. There were also many Little Golden Books on sale, and we bought a *Little Golden Picture Dictionary* and a Golden Storytime edition of *Jack and the Beanstalk*.

The last book that we bought was a PSS Surprise Book entitled *A Surprise for Your Eyes*, priced at $4.99. It is a book with a shiny, hard cover; thick, smooth paper; and bold illustrations. On each page there is a cut-out shape of an object that is a part of the picture. The first cut-out is of a butterfly with the blue showing through from the following page. "Do you see a big BLUE butterfly?" the child is asked. But as the page is turned the butterfly is gone and the blue can be seen as the color of the kite that flies in the sky. In this way, a pink birthday cake becomes a frilly dress, a green pickle becomes a frog, and a black boot becomes a penguin "in his best BLACK suit." The quality of *A Surprise for Your Eyes* was certainly worth the price, but we wondered about paying so much for a book in this particular location. Books for under a dollar were available in large numbers, making it easy for us to make a selection, but there were very few books in the five-dollar price range. This made us wonder if it would not be better for a parent who wished to spend this much on a book to go to a store that offered a wider selection of books in this price range. Bookstores would certainly offer a much wider selection of books, and they are generally of better quality than that offered in discount department stores.

Other department stores often have book departments in which children's books can be found, and although many of the books may be too expensive to buy on a regular basis, storewide sales can bring some of them within everyday reach instead of their just being books for special occasions. Sometimes department-store sales result in a wide selection of books in the five- to six-dollar price range, so it is worth a visit to see what you can find. But a broader variety of books is needed if children are to truly benefit from their collections.

Secondhand bookstores and thrift shops offer parents the opportunity to inexpensively add all sorts of books to their children's collections.

We visit secondhand stores and thrift shops regularly, and although there are times when the books that we find are too tired and worn to give to a child, there are other times when a pile of old books seems to be filled with delightful surprises. We have found long-out-of-print books filled with fragile illustrations, copies of Mother Goose that we have never seen before, and well-loved favorites in good-as-new dust covers that look as if they have never been opened, let alone read with a child. What a feast to take home for the family to share.

It can be fun to take children along when you go hunting for books in secondhand stores. Sometimes such outings can add a new dimension to a young child's view of literature. One small boy that we know spent his first visit to a secondhand bookstore looking for new books and was disappointed when he didn't find any. But his dad found several titles that he had read when he was young and he bought them to share with his son. The boy listened to the stories and was surprised to find that they were "great." His visits to secondhand bookstores became a hunt through dusty covers as old and sometimes dilapidated books began to offer the possibility of high adventure and mysterious happenings.

Other often unthought-of places where you can add to children's book collections are garage sales, rummage sales, and charity bazaars. One mother that we know has built a large collection of books for her daughter through regular visits to garage sales. And we know of another family who almost doubled their collection when by chance they were able to fill up supermarket bags with books that were being sold for a dollar a bag. They had gone to a book sale at a local church and bought many interesting titles, including some picture books, for less than a dollar each. Then, while they were browsing through the books that were heaped on trestle tables, they heard that the books that were left at the end of the sale were to be sold for a dollar a bag. The rest were to be taken to the dump. The family went back in the evening as much to "save" the books as to add new titles to their collection. It was a full-scale rescue mission as they filled bag after bag with books that they then bought for a dollar a bag. What a time they had when they got home! They piled the books up on the living room floor and spent the evening looking at them. Some of the books were not of much interest, and others were badly damaged. Many of the books, however, had been marked as high as three dollars at the sale but had been left as people had searched for less expensive titles. *Treasure Island*, *Gulliver's Travels*, and a book with the intriguing title *Being a Boy* were among the books that the family added to their collection.

Visits to bookstores well stocked in children's books can be an invaluable experience for both parents and children.

These days, bookstores are filled with the most extraordinary selections of high-quality paperback books. What is most delightful is that many of these books are copies of the lovely hardback books that were published last year or the year before that. Difficult decisions are made easy as your favorites become available at more affordable prices.

For parents, bookstores offer the opportunity to examine new books (and sometimes to be reminded of old favorites) that can be purchased for birthdays and other special occasions. Very often the suggestion of books for presents is welcomed by other family members, who may find it difficult to think of a suitable gift for a niece or nephew. And it seems from the families that we have spoken to that grandparents are often the ones who purchase children's books that are too expensive for the young family to buy.

For children, just the visual experience of walking into a bookstore can be breathtaking. They can see that books are important enough to line all of the shelves, and that they are more than just a sideline next to the peanut butter and jelly. It gives them an opportunity to feel important as they look at the books that have been written and illustrated just for them. The extraordinary illustrations of Maurice Sendak, Tomie de Paola, and Donald Crews entice children into the pages of books that watchful parents may buy. Many bookstores have places for children to sit where there are store copies that they can enjoy. And even if these books cannot be taken home right away, titles can be written down and saved for special times when gifts are given. But children need not be disappointed and have to leave the store empty-handed, for the displays of paperback books are every bit as exciting for them to choose from.

Talking about which books to buy can become a serious matter that demands the full attention of both parent and child. Sometimes these discussions become a tug-of-war as the parent urges the purchase of a "good" book while the child determinedly argues for a less worthy title, perhaps a book based on a TV cartoon show. Although some educators might not agree with us, we would support the idea of buying the book the child selects. The most important thing is for children to see books as pleasurable; the ill effects of a dispute may be greater than any possible ill effects of the comic book. In addition, children's tastes and preferences take time to develop. Children's choice of books, if allowed to grow, may be very different from what we might have expected. One boy that we know always opted for comic books when he went to a bookstore. He loved to listen to stories, but he never chose them for himself and he never read them on his own. During a visit to a local bookstore when he was eight years old he chose *The Guinness Book of World Records* in a paperback edition and bought it with some money that he had been given for Christmas. The book became a constant source of delight. He regaled his family with information about the longest recorded attack of hiccups, the largest recorded hailstone, and the heaviest cat. "What shall I look up?" became a favorite phrase. The book was taken on long journeys in the car and on vacations. Each year a new edition was given to him, and at the age of twelve he is still interested in the book. But as he has grown, books about space, rocks and minerals, and wildlife have become increasingly important to him. He still buys comic books and enjoys reading them, but it is his books on the natural sciences and the old edition of *The Guinness Book of World Records* that are scattered about the house, left on chairs where he has been reading them. Comics have become bathroom reading.

The public library is one of the best places for parents and children to find storybooks.

Even though we began this chapter by emphasizing the importance of building a child's personal collection of books, we do not want to underestimate the importance of the public library system. It is the least expensive way to expose children to the extraordinarily rich and varied number of books that have been written especially for them. It is in the library that children can "try books on for size." They have the opportunity to choose books that they would like to make temporary additions to their personal collections. They can then take them home, read them, and share them with other members of their family. If there is a special book that a child particularly enjoys, a parent may later buy a copy to add to the child's permanent collection.

We have spent many hours watching parents and children as they browse through the hundreds and sometimes thousands of books that are available in the children's section of the library. Indeed, watching them is an addictive pastime, and we have had librarians join us as we watched. Perhaps what has been most interesting has been our observation that children make *real choices* about the books that they want to take home. Children wander between the shelves with one special book tucked under their arm as they examine other works, or they sit in a favorite spot pulling out books that they pile on the floor before they show them to Mom or Dad and make a decision about which ones to take home. We have also observed that parents and children spend a lot of time *talking* to one another. They look at covers and turn the pages. Parents pull books off the shelves and show them to their children. At such times a to-and-fro takes place that is often fascinating to watch and rewarding to see.

However, from our discussions with parents we do appreciate that it can be frustrating and sometimes worrisome when children want to take home books that the parents would not have picked. It can be difficult for parents to give their children opportunities to make real decisions about the books that they read. One day Cullen talked to us about choosing books with five-year-old Sarah, and she explained that Sarah often wanted to take books home that she would never have chosen to share. She said that they got around the problem by looking at books together and then making separate piles of the books that they would like to read. Cullen went on to say that she was always surprised to find that most of the books that her young daughter picked were fun to read, and then, smiling, she added that she was not always so pleased with her own selections.

Many of the families with whom we have talked make visits to the library a weekly outing, and very often such visits are scheduled so that children can take part in the special programs that are offered in libraries. Storytelling is a regular event in many libraries, while films are often shown and craft programs given. Sometimes parents can attend with their children and enjoy the programs together, while at other times parents can use the time to look at the books on the Parents' Shelf, select books for themselves, or enjoy a moment of solitude as they sit in a quiet area and read the newspaper or browse through magazines. If visits are made to the library when no activities are scheduled for children, parents can use the opportunity to read one of the stories that they are thinking of borrowing or to put together one of the puzzles and talk about their day. One mother that we know can often be found playing with her daughter at the puzzle table. The other day, when we were talking to her, she told us that she had lost Becky in the library and had been frantic trying to find her. She ran upstairs to the main library calling Becky's name. "I'm here, Ma. I'm reading. I'm reading," Becky answered. Becky, who is three, was lying on a bench with her feet in the air. In her hands was a book. Becky continued reading while her mother browsed for more books. By making children feel that the library is an inviting and comfortable place to be, parents lay the foundation for the development of successful readers and writers as their children grow in the knowledge that the library is inviting.

So far in our discussion about the library we have not mentioned the librarians who provide all the services that children enjoy. Again, from our discussions with parents it would seem

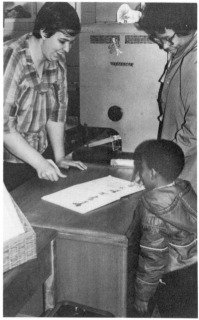

that some parents find it difficult to approach librarians and ask for help. This is especially so for parents who feel that they know very little about children's books. Sometimes they are not sure what questions to ask, while at other times they are concerned that their questions are trivial or even foolish. Perhaps part of their hesitation comes from the old-time notion of librarians as keepers of books rather than as supportive professionals who bring children and books together. Indeed, in many libraries librarians will not only help children find the books that are "just right" for them but they will also provide them with assistance with their homework and set up films so that children can listen through headphones as the pictures of their favorite story are displayed on a TV screen.

Part of the joy of visiting the library is having a library card of one's own. Libraries have different policies about the age at which children are allowed to have their own card. We have visited libraries that insist that children be in first grade before they are given a card so that they "know the value of books." Other libraries give children their first library card when they learn to write their own name, while still others give the gift of a library card to all the newborn babies whose families live within the vicinity of the particular library. Sometimes parents feel that obtaining a library card is important, and they are willing to visit other libraries in nearby towns to find one that will give a card to a very young child. This is a matter of personal choice, and it depends upon the accessibility of other libraries.

Taking care of the library books that children borrow is a major concern of many parents. There are many ways that parents can encourage their children to look after library books. Talking to their children about the consequences of torn pages and sharing with them the difficulties of trying to finish a story when there are pages missing helps young children appreciate the importance of caring for books. Some parents have told us that they keep all of the library books in a particular location or on a high shelf to ensure that they are not chewed or torn. Books belonging to the child that are "loved to pieces" can still be cared for, and the parent doesn't have to return them or perhaps pay for them, as they must when library books are due.

Book clubs and magazine subscriptions provide families with other opportunities to add to their children's personal collections.

For children, joining book clubs and having a subscription to a magazine offer the delightful prospect of packages arriving just for them. Many of the parents with whom we have spoken have, at one time or another, entered their children's name in a book club, and most of them have been enthusiastic about the books that they have received. Sometimes parents like the idea of receiving a book that they have not had to go out and buy. If a busy week has meant that there has been no time for a visit to a bookstore or library, then the postman bringing a book or a magazine can make a big difference to the time when parents and children read together. (To help you find out more about book clubs and magazines for your children, we have included a listing of these publications in an appendix at the back of this book.)

Perhaps it is here that we should also add a reminder that it is not only magazines for children that make excellent additions to children's collections, but also the enormous variety of magazines that parents buy and that children like to read. *Science '86* and *National Geographic* are enjoyed by children because of the extraordinary artwork and photography, but such periodicals as the Sears catalogue and the Green Shield stamp book also make excellent browsing materials for young children. They love to lie on the floor and go carefully through each page, naming objects that they know, asking about the names of others, and talking about still others that take their fancy. The toy sections of store catalogues often get special attention as even the very youngest of children seem to know that these sections are especially for them.

Sometimes the best books to share are those that are made by the children themselves.

In chapter 4 we emphasized the importance of encouraging children to write books for themselves. In this chapter we want to emphasize the importance of reading the books that they make, and of thinking of them as important titles in their personal collection. Books that are written by children should be stored with their other books on a low shelf. Where space permits, some of the covers should be facing out. Perhaps a few blank handmade books may be arranged with them so that a spare moment might become a time to write, to draw pictures, and perhaps to add another title to a much-loved collection.

6 WHAT SHOULD I LOOK FOR WHEN I'M CHOOSING BOOKS TO SHARE WITH MY CHILD?

Looking for books with young children is fun. It is a part of family life that offers immeasurable enjoyment for everyone. However, it can be a bit frustrating. There are so many books! Many of the parents with whom we have spoken are amazed at the wealth of materials available for young children. They become fascinated by the wide assortment of books, ranging from fanciful picture stories to more realistic stories about children who look and talk just like their own youngsters, to informational works on nature and technology. For some, the large selection is a mixed blessing: it is both a marvelous revelation and an overwhelming experience. But you don't have to be an expert in children's literature to choose books that you and your children will enjoy. The best way to learn about children's literature is to read it widely. The best way to learn about children is to talk with them about books and other things of importance to them. Your knowledge of both the books and the child's interests will develop as you go along. Indeed, for many parents, this becomes the fascinating part of it all. In this chapter we want to offer you a little help with this selection process by asking, "What should I look for when I'm choosing books to share with my child?" But first we want to take a quick look at who chooses the books.

Parents might begin by letting their children choose the books that appeal to them.

There are always some books that seem to be more attractive than others, that beg to be taken off the shelf and read by some small child. Book jackets are there to entice you. Once in small hands it will be opened and its stories will be shared. So open it! Look at the illustrations with your child, and read a few pages or perhaps just a paragraph or two. Then let the child simply select or reject it. It can be as simple as that.

If you buy the book, watch your child's reactions to the story when you read it and listen to the comments made by the other children in the family. It's a good way to learn about your children's tastes and interests as well as your own. Children have so many ways of letting us know what they like and dislike. Perhaps one of the most important things to remember in choosing books with young children is that it provides them with an opportunity to build tastes and personal preferences. This is especially true with young children, since they are relative newcomers to the world and have limited experience with books. Reading the books that they choose is therefore important.

Sometimes parents like to select the books that they share with their children.

Working parents might pick a book up on the way home at the end of the day, a shopping trip might include a visit to a bookstore, or an upcoming birthday might make an occasion of finding just the right book for a very special child. It might be the cover of the book that appeals to you, it might be the quality of the illustrations that you see when you open the book, or it might be the language that makes you want to turn the pages and buy the book. Sometimes it's the fact that the book is one you remember from your childhood that makes you rush home to share it with the family or with a particular child. You might find a book that a friend has mentioned to you, or perhaps you are attracted to a particularly beautiful counting book because one

of your children is counting all day long. In this way, book selection takes place. It is far from an exacting or burdensome task. It is neither scientific nor mysterious. Like most things relating to your children's growth, it is based on what appeals to your children and in this case, what appeals to you.

Although we have generally put children first and stressed how important it is that they have the opportunity to make *real choices* about the books they listen to and read, that doesn't mean storybook sharing should be limited to their selection. There is no reason why you can't choose books that you like and want to share. It is also important for young children to listen to a wide selection of stories and to hear a parent say, "I love this book," or, "This book is awful." In previous chapters we met Larry and his daughter Rachel. On one of the story reading tapes that Rachel's family made for us, Larry reads *Goodnight Moon* by Margaret Wise Brown. At the end of one reading, Larry says to Rachel, "I tell you, this *Goodnight Moon* book is just a lovely simple little book. If this woman, who died so young, had done nothing else but write this poetic book. . . ." There's a slight pause and Larry adds, "Real nice." Rachel says her own words and Larry responds, "You think so? Isn't that nice." Rachel was seventeen months old when this conversation took place with her dad. One could argue that she could not have understood what he was saying. But his love of the book comes through not only in what he says but in the caring way that he speaks and in the quiet moment that he shares with his little daughter. It is in this way that parents and children learn from one another. They learn about themselves and the books that they share.

Now that we have discussed who should choose books and why, let's focus upon the question "What should I look for when I'm choosing books to share with my child?"

Toy and board books are among the very first books that most children get to call their own.

Toy and board books encourage child participation and active use by virtue of their flaps, pop-ups, and laminated cardboard pages. Although there is some disagreement among educators as to whether they should be called toys or books, most parents agree that children enjoy them both ways. For the very young child, the element of surprise that comes when there is a hole to peek through or an unusual shape, flap, or lever to manipulate helps to extend the joy of the lively talk surrounding the text and pictures. Equally important, the pleasure of handling a book "all by myself" goes on long after Mom or Dad has gone to take care of other things.

In recent years, an increasing number of highly regarded authors and illustrators have lent their talents to producing what are often a baby's first books. The list of books below can serve as a benchmark of quality in the selection of children's first books. Many of them are toy and board books.

The Baby's Catalog by J. and A. Ahlberg (Little, Brown).
Betsy and the Doctor by G. Wolde (Random House).
The Chick and the Duckling by M. Ginsburg (Macmillan).
Have you seen my Duckling? by N. Tafuri (Greenwillow).
Marmalade's Nap by C. Wheeler (Knopf).
Max's First Word by R. Wells (Dial).
Miffy by D. Bruna (Price/Stern).
My Backyard by A. H. Rockwell (Macmillan).
Pat the Bunny by D. Kunhardt (Golden Books, Western).
What Sadie Sang by E. Rice (Greenwillow).
Where's Spot? by Eric Hill (Putnam).

Don't forget to include Mother Goose rhymes and verses.

Young children still love Mother Goose, and there is probably some truth to the warning, "When missed in early childhood, they are lost to the child forever." It is the rhythm and rhyme rather than the content of these verses that hold such delight for children. Childhood memories of singing and rocking to the verses apparently remain for a very long time. It is not uncommon to find nine- or ten-year-olds returning to the rhymes to read them on their own, perhaps with a sense of nostalgia or needed confirmation of control over their own ability to read for themselves.

Book of Nursery and Mother Goose Rhymes by M. de Angeli (Doubleday).
Mother Goose, illus. by M. Hoague (Harper and Row).
Mother Goose by T. Tudor (McKay).
The Real Mother Goose by B. F. Wright (Rand McNally).
The Tall Book of Mother Goose by F. Rojankovsky (Harper and Row).
Tomie de Paola's Mother Goose by T. de Paola (Putnam).

Picture storybooks make up a large proportion of the books shared with young children.

Picture storybooks come in every conceivable variety. Children love them largely because they love stories. Love of stories seems to be a natural part of being human; it starts very early in our lives and never leaves us. Whether we are young or old, whether it be Shakespeare or a television situation comedy, it is the story that captivates us. The best picture storybooks are those in which the text and pictures work together in close harmony to weave a tale. Young children enjoy stories about other children and about animals who behave like themselves. They enjoy humor expressed through words and pictures. Most children move with ease between make-believe and reality. Through listening to stories, looking at pictures, and talking with Mom or Dad, they

100

*What Should I
Look for When
I'm Choosing
Books to Share
with My Child?*

gradually develop their own sense of what is possible and what is not. As children mature, the books read aloud to them often include fewer pictures and more text. These illustrated books may contain chapters, which can serve as a guide for beginning and ending each family storybook reading session. Many of the books listed below are old favorites that have been around for generations. Others are equally loved, but are more recent titles. We think that they are all stories too good to miss.

Alfie Gets in First by S. Hughes (Lothrop).

Bright Farm and Me by J. Leech and Z. Spencer (Harper and Row).

Caps for Sale by E. Slobodkina (Addison-Wesley).

Corduroy by D. Freeman (Viking).

Crictor by T. Ungerer (Harper and Row).

Curious George by H. A. Rey (Houghton Mifflin).

Doctor De Soto by W. Steig (Farrar, Straus and Giroux).

Fables by A. Lobel (Harper and Row).

Goodnight Moon by M. W. Brown (Harper and Row).

Harry the Dirty Dog by G. Zion (Harper and Row).

Horton Hatches the Egg by Dr. Seuss (Random House).

I Can Do It by Myself by L. J. Little and E. Greenfield (Crowell).

The Little Engine That Could by W. Piper (Platt and Munk or Scholastic).

The Little Rabbit Who Wanted Red Wings by C. Bailey (Putnam).

Madeline by L. Bemelmans (Viking).

Make Way for Ducklings by R. McCloskey (Viking).

The Man Who Didn't Wash His Dishes by P. Krasilovsky (Doubleday).

Mike Mulligan and His Steam Shovel by V. L. Burton (Houghton Mifflin).

Millions of Cats by W. Gag (Putnam).

Mr. Gumpy's Outing by J. Burningham (Crowell).

Perez and Martina by P. Belpre (Warne).

Play with Me by M. H. Ets (Viking).

The Secret Hiding Place, by R. Bennett (World).

The Snowy Day by E. J. Keats (Viking).

The Story of Babar by J. de Brunhoff (Random House).

The Story of Ferdinand by M. Leaf (Viking).

Umbrella by T. Yashima (Viking).

A Very Special House by R. Krauss (Harper and Row).

Where the Wild Things Are by M. Sendak (Harper and Row).

Winnie the Pooh by A. A. Milne (Dutton).

101

*What Should I
Look for When
I'm Choosing
Books to Share
with My Child?*

Some traditional folktales and fairy tales should be included among the picture storybooks that you share.

Like the Mother Goose rhymes, folktales and fairy tales are a part of the literary heritage that is passed along from generation to generation. Fortunately, there is an abundance of folk literature available from places as diverse as Russia, Japan, Italy, Africa, and Germany. In some cases, you might find several different versions of the same tale to compare. For example, it is interesting to contrast the differences in text and pictures among various interpretations of "The Three Billy Goats Gruff" or "The Little Red Hen." You will find that many of these tales contain repetitive, predictable language that invites children to join in and chant as you read. The simple plots and language patterns of folktales also make them great for retelling by children and for acting out as well.

Arrow to the Sun: A Pueblo Indian Tale by G. McDermott (Viking).
Cinderella by M. Brown (Scribner's).
The Emperor's New Clothes by H. C. Andersen (Harper and Row).
The Fairy Tale Treasury by V. Haviland (Putnam).

102

*What Should I
Look for When
I'm Choosing
Books to Share
with My Child?*

Great Children's Stories (the classic Volland edition) by F. Richardson (Rand McNally).
The Little Red Hen by P. Galdone (Seabury).
Stone Soup, M. Brown (Scribner's).
The Turnip by J. Domanska (Macmillan).

A large number of children's books seek to convey an understanding of certain concepts or abstract ideas.

ABC and counting books fall into the category of books that communicate abstract ideas, and so do books that attempt to help children develop an understanding of time and space. These books should be selected as much for the pleasure of sharing the lovely illustrations, rhyme, or humor for which a particular book might be known as they are for any reasons associated with learning letters and numbers. The most important reason that children need to learn the names of letters and numbers is so that they can talk about them with others. Children who have fun with these kinds of books will return to read them on their own and begin to notice the letters and numbers in other contexts—a poster on a bus, a magazine on the table, or a discarded grocery list in the kitchen. Most often, they will begin to recognize the individual letters in their own names. Matthew will turn to the letter *M* and exclaim, "That's my name!" Sarah, who may have only thought of her name as one entire shape that starts tall and ends tall with some short squiggles in the middle, might begin to look at her name as having separate letters that make up the whole. Most important, we cannot stress enough the need to let children such as Matthew and Sarah have the joy of making these discoveries for themselves. As parents, our responsibility is to provide the means by which these discoveries can be made. Certainly, we may answer questions, add to the information in the book, and even offer gentle prompts when appropriate. But, probably most important, we are there to share in the joy of the child's very own discoveries when they happen.

The ABC Bunny by Wanda Gag (Putnam).
Anno's Alphabet: An Adventure in Imagination by A. Mitsumasa (Harper and Row).
Anno's Counting Book by A. Mitsumasa (Harper and Row).

103
*What Should I
Look for When
I'm Choosing
Books to Share
with My Child?*

Farm Alphabet Book by J. Miller (Prentice-Hall).
Farm Counting Book by J. Miller (Prentice-Hall).
The Guinea Pig ABC by K. Duke (Dutton).
More Than One by T. Hoban (Greenwillow).
My First Counting Book by L. Moore (Simon and Schuster).
1 Is One by T. Tudor (Rand McNally).
The Very Hungry Caterpillar by E. Carle (Putnam).

Beyond ABC and counting books are many other concept books that deal with a single abstract idea such as color, time, space, and size relationships.

ABC and counting books are, of course, not the only books that deal with concepts. There are also books that deal with such abstract ideas as color, time, space, and size relationships. There is even a book for young children about words. Still other informational picture books cover a wide range of more concrete subjects such as dogs, clocks, airplanes, and other topics of interest to young children. Sometimes the information is given in story form, with the story characters systematically exploring a topic as the reader eagerly accompanies them. At other times, the information may simply be offered in a straightforward, direct manner with pictures used to illustrate the various points being made. It is important for parents to be aware that informational books for children, as simple as they appear, must meet the same standards of accuracy and authenticity required of informational books for adults. These books serve as a major resource for helping you help your child find out about the world, and they are frequently referred to long after they are first read. Something said to the child, something experienced at play or on a trip, or the sharing of another book could trigger a reference or reflection to information originally encountered in these kinds of books.

Adventures of Three Colors by A. Tilson and T. Taylor (World).
Big Ones, Little Ones by T. Hoban (Greenwillow).
Brian Wildsmith's Puzzles by B. Wildsmith (Franklin Watts).
Did the Sun Shine Before You Were Born: A Sex Education Primer by
    S. Gordon and J. Gordon (Okpaku Communications).
Freight Train by D. Crews (Greenwillow).
How to Have Fun with a Vegetable Garden (Children's Press).
How You Were Born by J. Cole (Morrow).
It Looked Like Spilt Milk by C. Shaw (Harper and Row).
Look Again by T. Hoban (Macmillan).
My Visit to the Dinosaurs by Aliki (Harper and Row).
Sun Up, Sun Down by Gibbons (Harcourt).
Symbols by R. Myller (Atheneum).
We Read A to Z by D. Crews (Harper and Row).
When an Animal Grows by M. Selsam (Harper and Row).

Some picture books contain no words.

Some books have no words; the message must be interpreted through the pictures. These wordless texts are fun for very young children and for children in the early grades of elementary school, as the pictures stimulate both language and thinking. By looking carefully at the pictures, you and your child can tell the story or discuss the message in your own words. Children learn to study the pictures with care in order to tell what is happening, where it is happening, and what the characters might be thinking or saying. They use the information in the pictures to make inferences, which they translate as they talk to you. Occasionally, you might enjoy tape-recording your child telling a story from a wordless book. Or you might tape brothers and sisters making up a story together. The tapes are fun to play back as the pages are turned. We have listened to many tales told in this way, and we can always tell which children have listened to stories. They tend to use story language, such as "Once upon a time." They also tend to use more descriptive language and make the characters speak with expression. Of course, they are imitating those who have been reading with them.

The Bear and the Fly by P. Winter (Crown).
A Boy, a Dog, and a Frog by Mercer Mayer (Dial).
Changes, Changes by P. Hutchins (Macmillan).
The Good Bird by P. Wezel (Harper and Row).
I See a Song by E. Carle (Crowell).
Rosie's Walk by P. Hutchins (Macmillan).
The Snowman by R. Brigg (Random House).

If you were to ask, "Which kind of literature is least often read to children?" we would answer, "Poetry."

Our informal chats with parents seem to suggest that poetry is the kind of literature least often read to children. Beyond the stage of Mother Goose, poetry often gets neglected as families search for interesting stories to share. There may be a number of reasons for this. In some cases, parents may have unpleasant memories of forced memorization and recitation of poetry in school. Or they may have had so little exposure to poetry themselves that they simply do not think of it as something valuable for sharing with children.

We urge you to share poetry with your children on a regular basis. Occasionally you might wish to spend the entire storytime reading poetry selections. We often prefer to read one or two poems just before or after the sharing of a story. Favorite poems will soon be requested, and you will be amazed to find that children take great pride and pleasure in memorizing their favorite verses and refrains, something they seem to do with ease when it is of their own choosing.

All Together: A Child's Treasury of Verses by D. Aldis (Putnam).

106

What Should I
Look for When
I'm Choosing
Books to Share
with My Child?

A Child's Garden of Verses by R. L. Stevenson (Scribner).
Everett Anderson's Year by L. Clifton (Harper and Row).
Every Time I Climb a Tree by D. McCord (Little, Brown).
The Golden Treasury of Poetry compiled by L. Untermeyer (Western).
The Jumblies by E. Lear (Warne).
Nuts to You and Nuts to Me: An Alphabet of Poems by R. Solbert (Knopf).
Oxford Book of Poetry for Children compiled by E. Blishen (Oxford University Press).
Random House Book of Poetry for Children edited by J. Prelutsky (Random House).
Sniff Poems: A Scholastic "Scratch and Sniff" by J. Weil (Scholastic).
The Tamarindo Puppy and Other Poems by C. Pomerantz (Greenwillow).
When We Were Very Young by A. A. Milne (Dutton).

Some books are especially well suited to family sharing.

Obviously, you will want to choose books that are within your child's range of understanding, but don't be afraid to reach a little now and again. Children don't need to understand every word of a story in order to get a sense of the meaning. In families where children of different ages are sometimes read to at the same time, the books will frequently be geared to the older children. The younger children often enjoy these books, but at their own level of understanding. When they are older, they will return to these books with the enthusiasm of new listeners or readers creating new and more mature stories for themselves. The titles listed below can be enjoyed by children whose ages vary widely.

All-of-a-Kind Family by S. Taylor (Dell).
The Borrowers by M. Norton (Harcourt).
Charlotte's Web by E. B. White (Harper).
Cricket in Times Square by G. Selden (Farrar, Straus and Giroux).
The Elephant's Child by R. Kipling (Walker).
Family Under the Bridge by N. Carlson (Harper and Row).
Heidi by J. Spyri (Knopf).
The Lion, the Witch and the Wardrobe by C. S. Lewis (Macmillan).

Listen, Children: An Anthology of Black Literature by D. Strickland (Bantam).

Mama's Bank Account by K. Forbes (Harcourt).

Many Moons by J. Thurber (Harcourt).

Mary Poppins by P. L. Travers (Harcourt).

The Moffats by E. Estes (Harcourt).

Rootabaga Stories by C. Sandburg (Harcourt).

Treasure Island by R. L. Stevenson (Scribner).

The Velveteen Rabbit by M. Williams (Knopf or Holt).

L ook for books that encourage language play.

Some children's authors have a special talent for playing with the sounds, meanings, and even the appearance of language. Their creative use of language is a delight to children, since they, too, seem to have a natural talent for experimenting with words. Authors who play with the sounds of language often repeat language patterns in ways that evoke certain rhymes, rhythms, or sounds. Or they may use the sounds of the language to suggest a certain mood or feeling to the reader. Sometimes the actual size of the letters in the word will suggest a loud or quiet sound: large letters will be assigned to loud words and small letters to quiet words. Sometimes the arrangement of the print may give a clue to a word's meaning. At other times authors will play on the meanings of words or use puns, riddles, and nonsense words to engage the reader. Certainly, you will want to select some books that contain interesting uses of language to share with your children.

Amelia Bedelia by P. Parish (Harper and Row).

Chicken Soup with Rice by M. Sendak (Harper and Row).

A Chocolate Moose for Dinner by F. Gwynn (Dutton).

Eye Winker, Tom Tinker, Chin Chopper: A Collection of Musical Finger Plays by T. Glazer (Doubleday).

Fortunately by R. Charlip (Scholastic).

I Know an Old Lady by A. Braboff (Rand McNally).

One Old Oxford Ox by N. Bayley (Atheneum).

The Piggy in the Puddle by C. Pomerantz (Macmillan).

Rain Makes Applesauce by J. Scheer (Holiday).

Roar and More by K. Kuskin (Harper and Row).

108

*What Should I
Look for When
I'm Choosing
Books to Share
with My Child?*

A Scale Full of Fish and Other Turnabouts by N. Bossom (Green-willow).

Sparkle and Spin, a Book About Words by P. Rand (Harcourt).

The Tool Box by A. and H. Rockwell (Macmillan).

A Twister of Twists, a Tangler of Tongues by A. Schartz (Lippincott).

The Wedding Procession of the Rag Doll and the Broom Handle and Who Was in It by C. Sandburg (Harcourt).

There are books for special needs and special times.

Some books are specifically focused on a particular issue or problem. Such topics as fear of the dark, the challenge of sleeping over for the first time, and going to the dentist have been successfully broached in children's literature. Sharing an appropriate book with your child at a critical time may help to ease you both through a sensitive period in family life. For example, several books have been written about bringing a new baby into the family. Sometimes a child can be helped merely by knowing that other children have experienced the same kind of feelings.

Although most of these books deal with the ordinary emotions and feelings that are a part of every child's growing up, a little investigation will reveal that children's books have been written about almost every aspect of contemporary life. Books dealing

109

*What Should I
Look for When
I'm Choosing
Books to Share
with My Child?*

with death, divorce, and child abuse can now be found among the literature for children. If you are looking for a particular topic of this type, it might be wise to seek a librarian's help. Otherwise, if you should come across such a book and find that it is well written and the topic is of interest to you and your child, don't hesitate to read it even though it may not have immediate significance to the events or problems in your own lives. These books need not always be used to attack a certain problem. Indeed, the titles suggested below make good reading any time. The focused theme should simply be regarded as one more part of the ever-expanding knowledge that takes place through family storybook reading.

Alexander and the Terrible, Horrible, No Good, Very Bad Day by J. Viorst (Atheneum)—solving personal problems.

Annie and the Old One by M. Miles (Little, Brown)—death.

Benjie on His Own by Joan Lexau (Dial)—shyness and accomplishment.

Best Friends for Frances by R. Hoban (Harper and Row)—friendship.

Breakfast with My Father by R. Roy (Houghton Mifflin)—separation.

Crow Boy by T. Yashima (Viking)—loneliness, differences.

Curious George Goes to Hospital by H. A. Rey (Houghton Mifflin)—illness.

The Dead Bird by M. W. Brown (Young Scott Books)—death.

A Friend Can Help by T. Berger (Raintree)—divorce.

Frog and Toad are Friends by A. Lobel (Harper and Row)—friendship.

I Have a Sister, My Sister Is Deaf by J. W. Peterson (Harper and Row)—handicaps.

I Wish I Was Sick, Too by F. Brandenberg (Greenwillow)—illness.

Ira Sleeps Over by B. Waber (Houghton Mifflin)—fear and anxiety.

Leo the Late Bloomer by R. Kraus (Windmill)—accomplishment and growing up.

My Grandson Lew by C. Zolotow (Harper and Row)—grandparents, death.

Nanabah's Friend by M. Perrine (Houghton Mifflin)—fear and anxiety.

Nobody Asked Me If I Wanted a Baby Sister by M. Alexander (Dial)—new baby, jealousy.

Now One Foot, Now the Other by T. de Paola (Putnam)—illness.

101 Things to Do with a New Baby by J. Ormerod (Lothrop)—new baby.

On Mother's Lap by A. H. Scott (McGraw-Hill)—new baby, jealousy.

Someone New by C. Zolotow (Harper and Row)—growing up.

There's a Nightmare in My Closet by M. Mayer (Dial)—fear of the dark.

Whistle for Willie by E. J. Keats (Viking)—accomplishment.

William's Doll by C. Zolotow (Harper and Row)—sex stereotyping.

Will I Have a Friend? by M. Cohen (Macmillan)—friendship.

Youngest One by T. Yashima (Viking)—shyness.

Family storybook reading ends with hugs.

As we combed through the hundreds of books that we considered for inclusion on our list, there were some books that seemed to defy the usual categorization. We soon came to realize why these books were so very special. They are the perfect ending to this precious time of sharing. They end in hugs.

Ask Mr. Bear by M. Flack (Macmillan).

Farm Morning by D. McPhail (Harcourt).

Good As New by B. Douglass (Lothrop).

Little Bear by E. Minarik (Harper and Row).
Mother, Mother, I Want Another by Polushkin (Crown).
Mr. Rabbit and the Lovely Present by C. Zolotow (Harper and Row).
My Mother Is the Most Beautiful Woman in the World by B. Reyher
  (Lothrop).

111

*What Should I
Look for When
I'm Choosing
Books to Share
with My Child?*

Hug me, love me, and grow with me is the message that parents and children find hidden between the pages of the books that they share. Even the youngest of children can read this message and understand its meaning. Family storybook reading is a time when parents and children learn from one another as their lives come together in the stories that they read. We believe that this kind of experience is unique to the lives of families, and that it cannot be duplicated in any other way. For when parents and children read stories together, they create their own stories, original stories that are filled with the special kind of magic that all families can share.

APPENDIX

Several paperback book clubs are available through schools. The Scholastic Book Clubs are well known, but we would also encourage you to find out about the Trumpet Club. Three-quarters of the books offered through The Trumpet Club are Dell Yearling and Laurel-Leaf books.

Scholastic Book Clubs, 904 Sylvan Avenue, Englewood Cliffs, NJ 07632.
The Trumpet Club, P.O. Box 604, Holmes, PA 19043.

MAGAZINES FOR CHILDREN

Children's Digest. Stories, poems, science, nature, book reviews. Published by Parents Magazine Enterprises, Inc., Benjamin Franklin Literary & Medical Society Inc., Box 567B, 1100 Waterway Blvd., Indianapolis, IN 46206. 9 issues per year. (Ages 8–12)

Cobblestone: The History Magazine for Young Children. Articles, maps, poems, puzzles, crafts. Cobblestone Publishing, 28 Main St., Peterborough, NH 03458. 12 issues per year. (Ages 8–13)

Cricket. Artistic literary magazine for children, with monthly insert for parents. Open Court Publishing, Caris Corp., Box 100, La Salle, IL 61301. 12 issues per year. (Ages 8–12)

Ebony, Jr. Fiction, nonfiction, black history, crafts, games. Johnson Publishing Co., Inc., 820 S. Michigan Ave., Chicago, IL 60605. 10 issues per year. (Ages 6–12)

Highlights for Children. Fiction, nonfiction, science, crafts. Highlights for Children, P.O. Box 269, 2300 W. Fifth Ave., Columbus, OH 43216. 11 issues per year. (Ages 4–12)

Owl Magazine. Nature and science discovery. National Audubon Society and Owl Magazine, 255 Great Arrow Ave., Buffalo, NY 14207. (Ages 4–9)

Sesame Street. Stories, games, puzzles, nature. Children's Television Workshop, One Lincoln Plaza, New York, NY 10023. 10 issues per year. (Ages 3–6)

RESOURCES FOR PARENTS

American Library Association, 50 E. Huron St., Chicago, IL 60611. The following brochures are available:

- *The Caldecott Medal Books.*
- *Notable Children's Books.*
- *Books for All Ages*, a series of three pamphlets.

Babies Need Books by D. Butler. Atheneum.

A Child's Collection: The Definitive Catalog of Excellent Children's Books. A Child's Collection, 611 Broadway, Room 708, New York, NY 10012.

Choosing a Child's Book. Children's Book Council, 67 Irving Pl., New York, NY 10003. Pamphlet.

Choosing Books for Children: A Common Sense Guide by B. Hearne. Delacorte.

Family Literacy by D. Taylor. Heinemann.

For Reading Out Loud by M. Kimmel and E. Segel. Delacorte.

Helping Children Learn About Reading by J. A. Schickedanz. Pamphlet published by the National Association for the Education of Young Children, 1834 Connecticut Ave. NW, Washington, DC 20009.

The Read-Aloud Handbook by J. Trelease. Penguin.

Reading Begins at Home by D. Butler and M. Clay. Heinemann.

What Books and Records Should I Get for My Preschooler? Pamphlet published by International Reading Association, 800 Barksdale Rd., P.O. Box 8139, Newark, DE 19714-8139.

Why Children's Books? A Parent's Newsletter. Hornbook, 31 St. James Avenue, Boston, MA 02116. 4 issues per year.

You Can Encourage Your Child to Read. Pamphlet published by the International Reading Association, 800 Barksdale Rd., P.O. Box 8139, Newark, DE 19714.

CHILDREN'S BOOKS CITED

Brown, Margaret Wise. *Goodnight Moon*. New York: Harper and Row, 1947.

Bruna, Dick. *My Shirt Is White*. New York: Two Continents/ Methuen, 1975.

Buck, Pearl S. *Matthew, Mark, Luke and John*. New York: John Day, 1966.

Campbell, Rod. *Dear Zoo*. New York: Four Winds Press, 1982.

de Brunhoff, Jean. *The Story of Babar the Little Elephant*. Translated by Merle S. Haas. New York: Random House, 1933, 1960.

Eastman, P.D. *Are You My Mother?* New York: Random House, 1960.

Gackenbach, Dick. *A Bag Full of Pups*. Boston: Houghton Mifflin, 1981.

Grimm, Brothers. *The Bremen-Town Musicians*. As told by Patricia Martin Zens. Racine, WI: Merrigold Press, 1964.

Hayward, Linda. *When You Were a Baby*. A Golden Book. Racine, WI: Western Publishing Co., 1982.

Jack and the Beanstalk. Retold by Stella Williams Nathan. Racine, WI: Golden Press, 1973.

Klimo, Kate (ed.). *Animals in the Country*. New York: Simon and Schuster, 1982.

Koelling, Caryl. *A Surprise for Your Eyes*. A PSS Surprise book. Los Angeles: Intervisual Communications, 1981.

Kunhardt, Edith T. *Animal Quiz Book*. A Golden Book. Racine, WI: Western Publishing Co., 1983.

Little Golden Picture Dictionary. Racine, WI: Western Publishing Co., 1981.

Pinkwater, D. Manus. *Lizard Music*. New York: Dodd, Mead and Co., 1976.

Provensen, Alice and Martin. *My Little Hen*. New York: Random House, 1973.

Risom, Ole. *I Am a Puppy*. A Golden Sturdy Book. Racine, WI: Western Publishing Co., 1970.

Selden, George. *Chester Cricket's Pigeon Ride*. New York: Farrar, Straus and Giroux, 1981.

Sendak, Maurice. *Pierre: A Cautionary Tale in Five Chapters and a Prologue*. New York: Harper and Row, 1962.

————. *Where the Wild Things Are*. New York: Harper and Row, 1963.

Shecter, Ben. *Hester the Jester*. New York: Harper and Row, 1977.

Toys for Baby. A Whitman Book. Racine, WI: Western Publishing Co., 1966.

White, Wallace. *One Dark Night*. New York: Franklin Watts, 1979.

Zokeisa. *Things I Like to Eat*. New York: Simon and Schuster, 1981.

————. *Things I Like to Look At*. New York: Simon and Schuster, 1981.

————. *Things I Like to Play With*. New York: Simon and Schuster, 1981.

————. *Things I Like to Wear*. New York: Simon and Schuster, 1981.

In addition to the above, see also the lists of books given in chapter 6, which categorize volumes by subject.